Herzl

Herzl

———

Steven Beller

PETER HALBAN
LONDON

This paperback edition published in Great Britain by
Peter Halban Publishers Ltd
22 Golden Square
London W1F 9JW
2004

www.halbanpublishers.com

A CIP catalogue record for this book is available from the
British Library.

ISBN 1870015 90 8

Originally published in Great Britain
by Peter Halban Publishers Ltd
1991

Typeset by Computape Typesetting, North Yorkshire
Printed in Great Britain by
Mackays of Chatham, CPI Group

CONTENTS

FOREWORD TO SECOND EDITION

In the century that has elapsed since Theodor Herzl's death—on 3 July 1904—there has been a radical transformation of the place of Jews in the world, and in the nature of Jewish identity. Despite the brevity of his time at the centre of Jewish history (less than ten years from his Zionist 'conversion' to his death) Herzl, as the founder and leader of the Zionist movement, and hence the 'father of the state of Israel', arguably had more of an impact on this change than any other figure.

The last century has seen the Holocaust, but this evil and disastrous event has been followed in Jewish history by the creation of the state of Israel. Zionism and its achievement have created a revolution in Jewish self-understanding: most Jews in the world today regard themselves as Zionists, they see themselves in one way or another as part of a Jewish nation, and they regard Israel as the concrete expression of the Jewish people's national right to self-determination. This was not the case in 1904. The role that Herzl played in setting off this huge change in Jewish self-perception is discussed in this book. It is not as straightforward as often thought, for there was already a Zionist movement before Herzl came to his revelation in 1895, and the pre-existing strength of Zionist sentiment among Eastern European Jews partially explains Herzl's subsequent success. Yet Herzl's role in leading the movement was crucial. Given that role, and Israel and Zionism's central place in modern Jewish consciousness, the last hundred years of Jewish history could be called 'Herzl's century'.

Yet Herzl's Zionist legacy is now at a turning point. Israel, the *Judenstaat* of which Herzl wrote so prophetically in 1895, is in a state of crisis that goes to the very meaning of the state itself. Many Jews around the world look at Israel, searching as if in a mirror for their own Jewish identity, and they are often perplexed and disturbed at what they see. At this critical juncture in modern Israeli, and hence modern Jewish history, it is therefore important to remember the original inspiration of Zionism and the state that it founded. If we compare Herzl's original thinking and goals with the character of the current state of Israel, along with the position in which the global Jewish community now finds itself, the results show the continued relevance of Herzl today.

Herzl's thought and its Jewish character is the subject of this book, but it is appropriate to be reminded here of several aspects of his thought. Let us begin with Herzl's sense of what his *Judenstaat* was meant to accomplish. The over-arching goal of his Zionism was the creation of a state which the Jews could call their own, where they would not be a pariah minority but rather would be the 'normal' inhabitants of their nation-state, as Germans were in Germany, the French in France. In their own state, in other words, Jews would normalise themselves and gain the 'inner freedom' of a people that was not oppressed, either politically or psychologically. Part of this basic goal, however, was a much more idealistic one: the creation of the Zionist state might not have been for Herzl the messianic event foretold in the Jewish religious tradition, but it was intended as an opportunity for Jews to fulfil their traditional role as a 'light unto the nations', in secular terms. Herzl's vision of the Jewish state in both *Der Judenstaat* and the later *Altneuland* is one in which Jews seize the chance to become world leaders in technology, social and economic organization, and in attitudes to others and to 'the Other'. Jews in the new land would, above all, be tolerant of other groups for, as Herzl put it: 'We learnt tolerance in Europe.' If Jews were going to be 'normal', in other words, this was going to be a special, highly progressive, liberal and pluralist form of normality.

Herzl's Zionism had another aim that was central to his

whole idea: the creation of a Jewish state would, by relieving Europe of most of its Jews, cure the world of anti-Semitism. Herzl's vision was therefore one that rescued Europeans from themselves as well as Jews from anti-Semitism, and it was in this light that Herzl thought he could obtain what was to him the vital precondition of the success of his venture: the recognition and agreement of the international community to the Zionist enterprise and subsequent state. For without this agreement there could never be the peaceful conditions that would enable the Jewish state to flourish in the progressive and tolerant way that, in Herzl's eyes, was its very justification.

A hundred years on, how has Herzl's legacy fared? Many Israelis would no doubt agree with the idea that the existence of Israel and the experience of living in a Jewish state has created a Jewish normality that had never before existed. On the other hand, it could also be argued that changes in the West, such as the loosening and greater inclusiveness of national identities, and the development of pluralist thinking, have created a situation where Jews outside Israel can also feel the 'inner freedom' that Herzl yearned for. As for the idea of Israel as the Jewish expression of a humanistic ideal, Israelis have often tried very hard to live up to this calling, especially in terms of advanced social and economic forms of co-operation. Yet the conflict with the Arabs and, above all, the Palestinian people, always undermined the good intentions of the Zionist cause, and it is this conflict that is now threatening to distort the ethical character of Israel in ways that Herzl would have found loathsome. In defence of the current situation in Israel, and the Zionist rationale that has led to this point, circumstances were never very conducive to achieving a liberal, tolerant solution to the conflict and the potential for tragedy was present from the very start. It is worth noting that Herzl himself chose at first to ignore the fact that the Holy Land was not the sort of *tabula rasa* that he had wished for in his initial plan, and then later argued that the Palestinian Arabs would end up accepting the Jewish state because of the prosperity Jews brought, completely ignoring his own argument that, no matter what Jews did, they always brought anti-Semitism with them, if they were not in a state of their own.

The most tragic irony is that Israel, far from having cured the world of anti-Semitism, has itself become a target of anti-Semitism, and its policies, many would say, have actively exacerbated anti-Semitic sentiment in the Muslim world, and now, again, in Europe. That Israel has become the main focus of 'anti-Semitism' instead of being the means to eradicating it is, from Herzl's perspective, an ironic proof of Zionism's central failure—the failure to reconcile the Jewish people to the rest of the world community.

Yet Israel exists, and most Israelis and Jews want the Jewish state to succeed, not merely in terms of survival but also in the higher goals which the founders of Zionism set for it. By looking again at Herzl's Zionist thinking, its origins, its motivations, its dreams, its false assumptions and also its many insights, we can not only see the ways in which the Zionist enterprise has failed to live up to its progenitor's expectations, but also find hints and suggestions, such as in Herzl's emphasis on the need for international acceptance and agreement for instance, as to how it can be put back on track, so that the original dream of a Jewish people at peace with itself and with others can finally be realized. I hope that this book can aid in that quest.

Steven Beller, Washington DC, July 2004

CHRONOLOGY OF HERZL'S LIFE

2 May 1860	Theodor Herzl born in Budapest, Hungary.
3 May 1873	Herzl's 'Confirmation' (Bar Mitzvah)
7 February 1878	Death of Pauline, Herzl's sister; shortly thereafter family moves to Vienna.
September 1878	Herzl matriculates in the Law Faculty, Vienna University.
11 May 1881	Member of the 'Albia' Burschenschaft.
9 February 1882	Review of Dühring's *Die Judenfrage*.
March–April 1883	Herzl leaves 'Albia'.
5 August 1885	Herzl gives up practice as lawyer, for career as playwright and feuilletonist.
4 May 1889	Performance of Herzl's *Der Flüchtling* at Vienna's Burgtheater.
25 June 1889	Marriage to Julie Naschauer.
6 February 1891	Suicide of Heinrich Kana.
5 October 1891	Herzl appointed as Paris correspondent for the *Neue Freie Presse*.
26 January 1892	Death of Oswald Boxer.
Winter 1892/3	Herzl's coverage of the Panama Scandal; makes suggestions to Bacher and Benedikt, then Baron Leitenberger, on the Jewish problem.
April 1894	Herzl writes *Die Glosse*.
19 October 1894	Conversation with the sculptor Samuel Friedrich Beer in Paris.
21 October–8 November 1894	Herzl writes *Das neue Ghetto*.

April 1902	Herzl finishes *Altneuland*.
9 June 1902	Death of Herzl's father.
7 July 1902	Herzl before the Royal Commission on Alien Immigration, in London.
October 1902	Publication of *Altneuland* in Leipzig.
22 October 1902	Conversation with Joseph Chamberlain.
January–May 1903	The El Arish project.
Late April 1903	Chamberlain makes informal offer of Uganda.
8 August 1903	Interviews with Russian ministers, Plehve and Vitte.
16 August 1903	British make official offer of Ugandan territory.
23–28 August 1903	Sixth Zionist Congress, in Basel.
11–14 November 1903	Kharkov Committee meeting.
23–24 January 1904	Audiences with Victor Emmanuel III of Italy and Pope Pius X.
11–15 April 1904	Meeting of the Greater Action Committee in Vienna.
30 April 1904	Herzl ordered by doctors to take rest cure at Franzensbad, Bohemia.
3 June 1904	Herzl moves to Edlach, Lower Austria.
3 July 1904	Death of Herzl in Edlach.
7 July 1904	Burial in Vienna.
17 August 1949	Herzl's remains reinterred on Mt Herzl, Jerusalem.

ACKNOWLEDGEMENTS

I would like to thank the Master and Fellows of Peterhouse, Cambridge, for providing the initial funding to research this book; the Austrian government for the funding of a research visit to Vienna in early 1987; the Institut für die Wissenschaften vom Menschen, Vienna, for their hospitality over the years; and Jean Halpérin and Jerry Hochbaum, of the Memorial Foundation for Jewish Culture, who gave me the experience of the Nahum Goldmann Fellowship, from which I learnt a great deal.

I would also like to thank Glenda Abramson, Risa Domb, Nicholas de Lange, Lionel Kochan, Mark Geller, Nicola-Jane Moran, David Wolfson, and David Goldberg, all of whom, whether they know it or not, contributed to my writing on Herzl. I am further indebted to the Leo Baeck Institute of New York, whose library and archive I inhabited for many months, and whose staff were at all times remarkably helpful and friendly. One member, Diane Spielmann, deserves especial thanks for her unceasing readiness to listen and to offer advice. She was also kind enough to read and comment on a draft of the book, as were Moshe Sokol and David Sorkin. Their comments, along with those of Peter Halban and Arthur Hertzberg, have all helped to clarify and develop my ideas. Another reader, of many drafts, has been my wife, Esther Brimmer, to whom I owe particular gratitude, not least for enabling me to write this book. I am most grateful to all of the above, and others not mentioned who helped along the way. This book is dedicated, however, for their understanding and their example, to my parents.

INTRODUCTION

Theodor Herzl is one of the great figures in modern Jewish history. He is regarded as 'the father of Israel' for his decisive contribution to the foundation of the Zionist movement. Although it is true that there were Zionists, even 'Zionism', before Herzl, it was the drive and the political vision of the Viennese journalist turned national leader which made the disparate Zionist groups into a unified, and major, political movement. Herzl, with his book *Der Judenstaat* and his leadership of the movement from 1895 until his death in 1904, gave Zionism its goal and its organization, especially its congress— vital prerequisites for the eventual establishment of the state of Israel. As such, he had a profound effect on how modern Jews think, for solidarity with the state of Israel, the achievement of the Zionist dream, has become a dominant form of Jewish identity. Without Herzl, it can be argued, this transformation might never have taken place.

If Herzl has changed the way Jews think, he does not enjoy much of a reputation as a Jewish thinker, at least among Jewish intellectuals and scholars. One Jewish historian with Zionist sympathies jestingly said that a book on Herzl as a Jewish thinker should be very short, because Herzl was neither a thinker, nor really Jewish. Such a view, while it would baffle Jews brought up to regard Herzl as a legendary figure, is, I suspect, fairly widespread in Jewish academic circles. Herzl is seen as a great leader, a man of action, whose complex personality and remarkable life make him a much more suitable subject for the biographer's, even the psycho-biographer's, pen, rather than as a candidate to be taken seriously as an intellectual force. Even his 'great idea', of the Jews' need for a state of their own, has been deemed unoriginal, most commentators pointing out that the same idea had been arrived at by predecessors such as Leon Pinsker and, even earlier, Moses Hess. Herzl is valued more for what he did towards realizing the goal of Zionism, than for his thoughts on what that goal was, or should be. It is the leader, not the thinker, who is revered.

Part of the reluctance to view him as a major thinker stems from the embarrassed perception that the father of the Jewish state appears to have had a very tenuous contact with Jewish tradition and culture, as it is understood today. In recent years Herzl's thought has been seen, in Carl Schorske's controversial interpretation, as having its roots in Austrian liberalism and in German nationalism. Schorske has gone so far as to compare Herzl with Karl Lueger and Georg von Schönerer, the two leading anti-Semitic figures of *fin-de-siècle* Vienna. Amos Elon has emphasized the Viennese character of Herzl's thinking. William Johnston has seen him as a Hungarian thinker, Joseph Adler saw him as a 'new humanist'. It has proved difficult, however, to make much of Herzl as a Jewish thinker in any straightforward sense. His pre-Zionist years were, famously, devoid of any significant Jewish content. He never had a very great affinity with the formal content of traditional Jewish life. Even after his Zionist conversion he remained in his way of thinking on a different wavelength from such plainly Jewish thinkers as Ahad Ha'am, or even Martin Buber.

Nevertheless, in his way, Herzl was as much a 'Jewish thinker' as these august figures. It is just that he came from a different tradition, the liberal Jewish tradition of Central Europe, which was much more intimately linked with Western culture than that of its Eastern European Jewish counterpart. It is the latter which has come to predominate in our understanding of what it means to be 'Jewish', and a 'Jewish thinker', and it can well be argued that this Eastern European tradition preserved much more of the substance of traditional Jewish culture and thought. Yet the modern

Central European Jewish tradition, more abstract perhaps, has had an enormous effect not only on Jewish modernity, but on modern culture and thought generally. Herzl was very much a product of this tradition.

In his thought, and especially through the way it developed, can be traced the strong influence of what has been called the 'ideology of emancipation': the system of thought which evolved in the wake of the *Haskalah*, or Jewish Enlightenment, to effect the integration of Jews into the modern world of Central Europe. It will be the contention of this book that Herzlian Zionism is not so much a realization of Austrian liberalism, or German nationalism, or a Hungarian utopia: it is the attempt to fulfil the promise of Jewish emancipation, if not in Europe, then in a state of Jews on their own. As a super-emancipationist, Herzl shows himself to be firmly in a major current of modern Jewish thought.

Once one sees Herzl from this perspective, he becomes not only an interesting historical figure, but a thinker who still has much to say to our world, and especially to the movement which he led, and the state which he did so much to help make possible. It is time to take Herzl seriously again as a thinker, and moreover as a Jewish thinker. In these days when so much soul-searching is taking place about the character of Israel, he offers, as we shall see, a liberal version of Jewish identity and the Jewish state which is perhaps more relevant now than ever before.

Whether one can learn from Herzl the thinker or not, and I think many could, and should, the story of how he came to Zionism, how he combined in it so many aspects of his thought, and how he dealt, or did not deal, with the movement which he discovered already in existence, is in itself a remarkable tale. Study of his thought reveals a man between West and East, between liberalism and nationalism, with an admiration of the values of aristocracy as well as technocracy, at the centre of Viennese intellectual society, yet an outsider, and a Jew whose Jewishness was first an embarrassment before it became his life's purpose. He is, in other words, a fascinating case study of the conflations, conflicts and complexities in a thinker of *fin-de-siècle* Central Europe.

Above all, he proves to be, in so many ways, characteristic of the group into which he was born, and among whom he was raised and lived: the Jewish bourgeoisie of late nineteenth-century Central Europe. It is within the context of that Jewish bourgeoisie that Herzl is most easily understood, for there lie the roots of the problems which he tried to solve through Zionism—and the roots of the ideal solution which he came to propose.

I

LIVING IN THE NEW GHETTO

Theodor Herzl's life before Zionism was typical of his generation of Central European Jewry, both in its form and its great complexity. His subsequent 'conversion' to Zionism, which he at first thought to be his own invention, has often presented a puzzle to his biographers, for it seems hard to understand how such an apparently well-assimilated person, who had successfully established himself as a well-known writer, was motivated into inventing a Jewish cause which seemed to negate his whole previous existence. In many ways, however, Herzl's pre-Zionist years (the bulk of his life), can be seen as only too effective a preparation for his later decision. Herzl could recognize the ways in which the emancipation and assimilation of Jewry had failed, because all he needed to do was call on his own experience. His life in Pest, in Vienna, and then in Paris gave him ample material to construct his later theories. Not only was his life a model of the complications, and hence the tensions, of being a Jew in Central Europe; his later vindication of his Jewish identity was to a large extent the response to the fact that the earlier Herzl had represented not so much a model of Central European Jewish self-understanding, as a near-pathological, self-hating version of the same. Herzl came to see the world of emancipated and assimilated Jewry in which he had grown up, and in which he so successfully operated, as a new ghetto with now invisible walls, which, for the sake of their self-esteem and sense of honour, the Jews had to escape. Zionism was the attempt to break down the ghetto walls once and for all.

Herzl was born in Pest in 1860, in a Hungarian state which was in the throes of national revival.[1] His father, a successful businessman and banker, originated from the military border district on Hungary's southern frontier. His mother was the daughter of Pest Jews who had come to the city from Moravia, the Austrian province to the north-west, fifty or so years before. Both parents were fairly typical products of the modernization of Jewry which had been undertaken under the auspices of the *Haskalah*, the Jewish Enlightenment. They sent their son Theodor to the Jewish primary school. At an early age Herzl would thus, through his school and his family, have imbibed the basic tenets of the ideology of emancipation. This ideology, which was the product of the struggles of Central European, especially German, Jewry for their emancipation, put its hopes for the liberation of the Jews in Enlightened and liberal theories of the state; at the same time it saw the necessity of Jews to reform themselves, to leave their former ways of beggary and usury, and other-worldly religious study, and instead concentrate on secular education and respectable economic pursuits; in other words, Jews were to become good citizens in order to deserve to be recognized as such.[2] (Full equality of rights for Jews in Hungary was only granted in 1867.)

Herzl's father was a somewhat ambivalent, if successful, example of this transformation, having become a respected and very rich banker—still, however, associated with money. That other Jews had not successfully transformed themselves despite emancipation was something which was to prey upon Herzl's mind in later life.

In 1870, Herzl, who had evinced an early interest in technical subjects (an early hero was Ferdinand de Lesseps, the builder of the Suez Canal), was sent by his parents to a secondary modern school, which emphasized more practical and technical subjects than the classical Gymnasium.[3] As is the case with many children, however, his earlier enthusiasm gave way to another, which was to prove much longer-lasting: his ambition to be a writer. Herzl's disenchantment with his new school may have had something to do with anti-Semitism among his Hungarian classmates and teachers, as he later reported, but the fact that in 1874 he had become the president of a juvenile literary society, Wir, is probably more important in explaining his poor performance at school, for he now devoted a great deal of his time to writing. Herzl, no longer so suited to, or keen on, technology, now fancied himself as a writer, and the way to acquire the necessary education for this august role led through the Gymnasium. So in 1876 Herzl entered the Evangelical Gymnasium in Budapest, a Hungarian-speaking school whose pupils, despite the denominational character of the school, were in a large majority Jewish. After his brief experience of a non-Jewish milieu, Herzl now entered an acculturated but socially Jewish milieu, which paralleled closely that of his parents and was prototypical of the predominantly assimilated but Jewish milieux in which he moved for most of the rest of his life. He had also acquired his life's goal, to be a writer.[4]

There was still a question at this stage of which language he would write in. Both of Herzl's parents were German-speaking. His mother was an especially warm admirer of German literature and culture, and she seems to have passed on her devotion to German letters to her son. This Germanophilism has often been taken to mean that Herzl grew up in an anti-Hungarian—because pro-German—family atmosphere, a belief also encouraged by the mature Herzl, who would emphasize his German upbringing and his early alienation from things Hungarian. The truth, as is often the case with Herzl, is somewhat different from his own account. Research into Herzl's childhood has shown that, as with many liberal Jewish families in Pest, the family's admiration of German culture did not necessarily conflict with support for Hungarian liberalism. The teenage Herzl was as good a writer in Hungarian as he was in German. Jewish families such as the Herzls were developing a bilingualism in line with their German Jewish tradition and their support for the liberal forces in their state, which were predominantly Hungarian.[5]

If he had stayed in Pest Herzl's Hungarian identity, which he was fast acquiring as a teenager, might well have predominated over his German one. The issue was decided in favour of a German identity when he and his parents moved to Vienna in 1878, after the death of Herzl's sister Pauline. It is sometimes thought that the Germanophile Herzls moved to Vienna to rescue themselves from a Budapest where Hungarian was rapidly overcoming German as the dominant language, and that Herzl thus found it easy to fit into the strongly German nationalist milieu which awaited the new law student at Vienna University. Yet Herzl's German identity was, at least initially, not as fixed as one might have thought. His university records show him claiming German as his mother tongue in his first semester in the legal faculty in 1878, which one would expect. What is surprising is that in the next semester his mother tongue has become 'Hungarian', and remains so until the summer semester of 1881, when it reverts to German. For two of his student years Herzl seems to have thought of himself as Hungarian.[6] Perhaps this explains why, as a member of the Akademische Lesehalle from 1879, he seems initially to have taken a pro-Austrian stance, against the German nationalist radicals.

The change back to German in the spring of 1881 coincided, however, with his joining the Burschenschaft 'Albia', from which point he seems to have prided himself on his German nationalist identity and accompanying social standing, as Arthur Schnitzler so graphically described in his memoirs.[7] It was perhaps the fact that this German identity was so new, and so questionable, that made Herzl now so intent on denying any affinity with Hungarian matters.

If he had problems with his identity as Hungarian or German, which he eventually solved to his own satisfaction by becoming fully German, this solution proved no solution at all, and only brought him greater problems. That he would have been naturally attracted to a German nationalist point of view is not surprising. It offered great social prestige to belong to such a Burschenschaft, and Herzl was at all times in his life attracted to social prestige. Furthermore, as the student careers of many Jewish figures of Herzl's generation show, the German nationalist ideology, a threat though it be to the integrity of the Habsburg Monarchy, was very popular among Jewish bourgeois youth. Indeed many of the German nationalist student leaders were Jewish, including Victor Adler, the future socialist leader, and Heinrich Friedjung, later a prominent (German) liberal historian. Others attracted to the movement were Gustav Mahler and, if fleetingly, Sigmund Freud.[8] That Herzl, even in Budapest, had had leanings towards an admiration of all things German is evidenced by the fact that he wrote a pro-Bismarckian poem in his mid-teens, and that it was Bismarck who replaced de Lesseps as his hero. Stories of German chivalry enjoyed in his youth presaged a lifelong admiration, one might almost say fixation, with the virtues of the Prussian nobility. German nationalism, once decided upon, did seem a sensible option for a young Pest Jew, immersed by his mother in the German classics, with ambitions to be a writer, a 'deutscher Schriftsteller', only newly arrived in the Habsburg capital, and with admiring eyes fixed on the newly emergent and triumphant German Reich.[9]

The problem was that the German nationalist student movement was anti-Semitic. Herzl must have been aware of this from the start, for there were anti-Semitic demonstrations by German nationalist students in Vienna as early as 1876. Nevertheless, a young Jew such as Herzl could see this anti-Semitism as not so much a rejection of himself, as of those money-grubbing, uncultured Jews who had not integrated themselves properly into German culture. In other words, he could view this as a cultural anti-Semitism with which he could agree. Had not the ideology of emancipation made it the responsibility of Jews to reform themselves so that they deserved citizenship? Was this protest against Jews who had not done their part to fit in as proper Germans not justified? That not all German Nationalist Burschenschaften rejected

Jews out of hand is evidenced by Herzl's own admittance to 'Albia' in 1881. He, at least, seemed to be an acceptable Jew.

This did not last long, however, for soon, as the movement radicalized, the definition of who was German became more exclusive; cultural anti-Semitism was replaced by a strictly racial anti-Semitism. Within student circles the chief cause of this shift was the changing stance of the emerging leader of German Nationalism in Austria, Georg von Schönerer, whose electoral campaign in 1882 used the slogan 'Was der Jude glaubt ist einerlei, in der Rasse liegt die Schweinerei.' (What the Jew thinks is irrelevant; the baseness lies in the race.) With this racial anti-Semitism there was no longer a place in German Nationalism for any young Jew, not even for former leaders such as Victor Adler, and certainly not for an ex-Hungarian such as Herzl.[10]

Herzl was made to confront this racial anti-Semitism not in politics, but rather in his favourite sphere: literature. In the space of two days in February 1882 Herzl wrote in his diary reviews of two books which dealt with the Jewish question. The first was Wilhelm Jensen's *Die Juden von Cölln*, written in 1869. Herzl saw this as a sympathetic account of Jews as members of a noble yet, for him, degenerate race. Thinking very much in the racial vogue of the time, and echoing his hero Bismarck, Herzl opined that the Jews needed to be racially mixed with those in whose midst they lived (Germans) to improve the breed. At this point his ideal was 'a cross-breeding of Western and Oriental races on the basis of a common state religion'.

That other consequences could be drawn from such racial thinking, however, was made brutally plain to Herzl when the next day he picked up the book which was the latest word on the Jewish question, Eugen Dühring's *Die Judenfrage*. This was, for Herzl, an 'infamous book'. What most troubled him about it was that it pointed out many faults in Jews which Herzl himself saw—indeed at one point Herzl acknowledges that what Dühring has to say about the Jewish lack of ethical seriousness should be read by every Jew—but left them with no hope of remedying these faults. This was because Dühring explained everything in the racial terms Herzl had dabbled with himself the night before, and drew the conclusion that this racial inferiority, the cause of the Jews' love of usury and their perversion of German culture, meant that Jews, instead of being racially integrated into German society (Herzl's ideal), would have to be excluded from all professions and all occupations, from German society generally. The final straw for Herzl was that Dühring attacked Ferdinand Lassalle, a Jew, fighter for social justice, and ardent German patriot, and thus a role model for Herzl as he was for many other Jews of that generation. Even Lassalle was now no longer a German; this conclusion must have been a profound shock for Herzl.[11]

Dühring's book would not have been so problematic if Herzl could have regarded it as the work of a crank. Unfortunately he was unable to do so because too many of his colleagues at the university took thought such as Dühring's seriously. This was made evident in the episode which brought Herzl's break with his student German nationalism. Shortly after the death of Wagner, who was not only anti-Semitic but also a culture hero of the German nationalist students, a sort of wake for the great composer was held in early March 1883 by various student bodies, including, it would seem, 'Albia'. Herzl, by now an 'inactive' member of the fraternity, did not attend, but a fellow member, Hermann Bahr, did. He gave a speech at the meeting which, by all accounts, reeked with anti-Semitism. Certainly the report on the night's events was enough to prompt Herzl to seek an 'honourable discharge' from 'Albia' in protest. Even if he had not been Jewish, he stated, he would have felt bound by his love of freedom to resign. As it was he carried with him the burden of 'Semitism' and would, in the light of recent events, never have considered joining 'Albia' in the first place. His parenthetic comment that when he had joined, a mere two years before, the word 'Semitism' had not been invented, was laden with an awful irony, for it showed just how much his attempt at a truly German identity had been hijacked by events.[12]

This by no means meant that he had given up his attempt to be recognized as a German writer, to fulfil the ambitions of his youth. In some ways the rejection by a large number of his (non-Jewish) peers probably spurred him on to achieve artistic recognition, and thus social acceptance, through his writing. In the next decade of his life Herzl paid little overt attention to his Jewish identity, and instead concentrated on being a writer. While studying for his law degree he continued to submit feuilletons for various competitions and to various newspapers, with some success but not much. Once he had graduated as a doctor of law he tried his hand at practising law, first in Vienna and then in Salzburg. Yet his heart was not really in it. Later he was to claim that he decided to give up his legal career because he could never have progressed far in a judicial hierarchy closed to Jews who did not convert. Perhaps this consideration did play a role: for a man as eager for fame as Herzl evidently was, any obstacle to upward mobility was unwelcome. A more likely explanation, however, is that, as the son of devoted parents who were rich enough to finance frequent trips abroad and were prepared to let their son fully develop his God-given literary talents, he preferred the excitements of the literary life and undoubted public fame to the drudgery of court proceedings.

From 1885 until 1891, therefore, he pursued a career of playwright and freelance writer-journalist. The irony of this was that such a career was about the most 'Jewish' career one could follow in late nineteenth-century Vienna, and the 'Jewish press' increasingly the target for anti-Semitic attacks. If, as Dethloff has cogently argued, Herzl's lifelong ambition to be a successful 'deutscher Schriftsteller' was a means to achieve social recognition despite being a Jew, it had become, by the time he did achieve success, just another 'Jewish' career.[13] What is more, despite achieving his life's ambition of having a play of his, *Der Flüchtling* (The Refugee), performed at the Burgtheater in Vienna, the premier stage in the German-speaking world, his career as a playwright never really took off, for all his many efforts to achieve the lasting success and fame which he craved.[14] Instead he became known as a talented feuilletonist, the writer of light, elegant essays with a touch of irony, often dealing with a serious theme, but never too deeply. This feuilletonistic tradition, imported from France, had become very strong in Viennese journalism. The style was generally modelled on Heinrich Heine, and one of its greatest Viennese exponents had been Daniel Spitzer. By 1890 it was regarded as one of the most typical products of the 'Jewish press'; this was something hard to deny, as many, if not most, of the Viennese practitioners of the literary form were of Jewish descent.

Herzl in these years is often seen by his biographers, most especially by Amos Elon, as having become a typical, almost archetypal, Viennese—a dandy, prone to the artistic pose of quiet melancholy, to an emphasis on display and symbol, fascinated by the world of dreams, and obsessed with the splendours of noble rank. The great theatricality of his approach to life has often struck commentators as a Viennese quality.[15] There is ample evidence that Herzl in some ways did indeed possess all these qualities, but it seems to me much more problematic to attribute these facets of his character to his 'Viennese' background. No doubt 'Theodor Viennensis' did his best to fit into his adopted home, and his pursuit of literary fame was largely motivated by such considerations. On the other hand the fit achieved was far from as neat as first appears, indeed it shows just how far Herzl was from being a 'typical' Viennese, and how far his Jewish background got in the way.

Even the Viennese derivation of his theatricality, on which most accounts agree, is somewhat open to question. Herzl was already, as a young man in Budapest, prone to flights of dramatic imagination, and this was what encouraged him in seeking to become a playwright long before he ever came to Vienna. That he was to think in dramatic terms when formulating his ideas on a state for the Jews and on Zionism as a political movement is quite clear. As a playwright, however, it is surely not that surprising that he used his dramatic skills when he entered the political realm.[16] Furthermore, as a

9

playwright Herzl was eminently unsuccessful—in Vienna. In his most 'Viennese' role, as a man of the theatre, Herzl's writing did not chime well with Viennese taste. This is understandable, for his plays tended to be clever, intellectual satires on high society, which, as the Burgtheater star Ernst Hartmann intimated, lacked human warmth. Drama, admitted Herzl at a later date, was not his true métier.[17]

Herzl was also plainly a dandy, an aesthete and a snob, fascinated by aristocrats and ideas of chivalry; but then so were many of the sons of parvenus all over Europe. This was not a phenomenon confined to Vienna. Moreover the nobility which was Herzl's ideal was not the Austrian aristocracy, for which he at times expressed a certain contempt, but rather the Prussian Junkers, from which his national hero, Bismarck, had sprung. Herzl also respected the principle of the duel, as a way to preserve 'honour' in society, but he seems to have regarded this as a French form of sophistication, not an Austrian one.[18]

Another apparently Viennese habit was his emphasis on dreams, most famously in the afterword to *Altneuland*, where he talks about the way reality is based on dreams, and then returns to them. Yet Herzl's usual meaning of the word 'dream' is not concerned with what we experience in our sleep, but is rather the idea of dream as wish, in the waking state. That is to say it is shorthand not for some Baroque sense of the unreality of life, but rather for the formulation of concrete wishes, such as, for instance, the 'dream' which Jews have had for two thousand years, to return to the Promised Land. Herzl, in this instance as in so many others, reveals himself as more liberal bourgeois and practical, perhaps more 'Hungarian', than one might think at first acquaintance, or from his biographers.

He was far more at odds with his Viennese environment than he at the time, or others later, were willing to admit. There was always the air of an outsider about him. In this context it is significant that, although he was resident in Vienna from 1878 until his crucial stay in Paris in 1891, he was often absent from the city. His parents financed trips all over Europe from 1883 on, and it was his travel feuilletons—from Italy in 1887, and the Pyrenees in 1891—which really made his name.[19] Part of what made him attractive to a Viennese readership was his European cosmopolitanism, his conveying to them a sense of the outside world, that which was not Vienna.

In this constant moving around the European continent, Herzl anticipated the peregrinations of another famous Viennese figure of a later generation, and a great admirer of his, Stefan Zweig. A few months before his death Herzl met Zweig in Vienna, and engaged him in conversation. He encouraged the young writer to continue his travels abroad, for which he was already well-known. 'Everything I know,' confided Herzl, 'I learnt abroad. Only there does one get used to thinking in distances. I am convinced, that here I would never have had the courage to formulate that first conception. Somebody would have nipped it in the bud before it had a chance to grow. But thank God, when I brought it here, it was already complete, and they could do nothing but cock a leg.' Zweig added that Herzl then spoke 'very bitterly' about Vienna.[20] In his frustration with his adopted city, one might say, Herzl was very Viennese, as he was, in a way, in his inferiority complex towards Germany and the Prussian nobility, and even in his admiration for things French and English. Such a negative identity, however, is quite different from the picture of the Viennese Herzl which is usually presented.

In another sense he was typical of the city, not so much as a Viennese, but rather as the son of the Viennese Jewish bourgeoisie.[21] He combined, as we have briefly seen, a very negative image of Jews and a powerful drive to assimilate into the 'German' nation, with a career and life pattern which was very Jewish. He pursued his career as a writer and journalist through various contacts of his father and others, and thus inevitably found himself in a cultural milieu which was still heavily Jewish. This did not chime at all well with his contempt for Jews less acculturated than himself. On a trip to Berlin in 1885, for example, reporting to his parents on a social event he had attended, he could remark: 'Yesterday there was a grande soirée at Treitel's. Thirty or forty ugly little Jews and Jewesses. Not a very refreshing sight.'[22]

At the same time he was a most loyal son, which put a limit on the degree to which he was prepared to assimilate. In 1886, when asked by Heinrich Friedjung, another German nationalist Jew, to contribute further feuilletons, but under a pseudonym that would be less Jewish-sounding, Herzl refused point-blank to give up 'his father's name'.[23] Judaism may have been, as another Viennese Jew, Theodor Gomperz, once remarked, only 'un pieux souvenir de famille', but this fact still made it a significant barrier to full assimilation. Furthermore, although he did have Gentile friends, such as, of all people, Hermann Bahr, his closest friends in these years were two Jews, Heinrich Kana and Oswald Boxer. Admittedly the woman whom he chose to be his wife was both blonde and blue-eyed, just like the heroines of the romantic tales of his youth. Julie Naschauer was, however, also Jewish, and moreover from an originally Hungarian Jewish family of nouveaux riches, precisely the kind of people who symbolized to Herzl all that was distasteful in Jews. The tensions in his identity at this time perhaps make it understandable that, having married a Jewish woman, whom he grew to hate, he then did not have his son Hans, born in the summer of 1891, circumcized.[24] Herzl thus lived a life in which he tried to ignore his Jewishness, was dismissive or contemptuous of his religion and his fellow Jews, and yet conformed very much to type: a Viennese Jewish bourgeois, with Jewish friends, a Jewish wife and a Jewish career.

Nor did he escape being on occasion reminded of his Jewishness. In one of his Italian feuilletons of 1887 the Rome ghetto caused him to remark on the way attitudes to Jews had, or had not, changed since the days of the ghetto, so that now Jews were not despised for their religion, but rather for their crooked noses and being rich, even when they were poor.

In 1888 he was directly confronted with anti-Semitism by having 'Hep! Hep!'* shouted at him in a Mainz pub.[25] In 1891 his friend Heinrich Kana committed suicide, an event which Herzl later claimed moved him to start thinking about a novel, *Samuel Kohn*, based on Kana's tragedy, which would be concerned with the sufferings of poor Jews due to an anti-Semitism largely caused by the actions of their rich fellow Jews.[26] The hero would only find his pride again in the achievement of his suicide. A few months later, in one of the Pyrenees feuilletons which made him a star, Herzl described a sick man's reaction to not having been cured at Lourdes: 'He sighed like a Jew!'[27] On the brink of finally making it as a writer, of feuilletons if not of plays, Herzl could still not shake off the fact of his Jewishness. As he was to intimate in a play he wrote shortly before his Zionist revelation, he was still living in a ghetto, even if it did now have invisible walls.

* Of medieval origin and probably short for *Hyrosolima est perdita* (Jerusalem is lost).

2

PARISIAN
PREMONITIONS

The Pyrenees feuilletons gave Herzl his great opportunity: he was offered the post of Paris correspondent of the *Neue Freie Presse*, by far the most prestigious Viennese newspaper, indeed the leading newspaper of Central Europe. In his Paris years Herzl matured greatly; and he began to realize how the world really worked, above all what politics was about. Having affected to despise the political world, he was now forced to confront the goings-on of the Palais Bourbon, and get to grips with reality. What he found repelled him, but fascinated him at the same time. Instead of the solid liberal, democratic structure which he had expected, Herzl found a system which seemed to run on corruption and deceit, and appeared on the verge of breaking up entirely. These were, after all, the years of anarchist outrages, of the Panama crisis, the rise of socialism and of anti-Semitism, and the Dreyfus trial. All this undoubtedly undermined what faith he may have had in the eventual triumph of liberalism, and thus Jewish emancipation and assimilation. It may also have been the case that his knowledge of Austrian circumstances, especially his experience of Schönerian nationalist politics, led him to have less confidence in the French political system than it might have merited, in the long term. His perceptive analysis of Maurice Barrès as an artist politician on the verge of a totalitarian politics of violent nationalism might well have been helped by his knowledge of Schönerer's antics a few years earlier.[1]

What Herzl acquired in Paris was a great interest in politics and an increasing concern for the Jewish question. Writing to a friend in May 1895, Herzl claimed that, in Paris, 'I entered the political world, and whether I liked it or not I learnt to see the matters of this world quite differently. At the same time I gained a freer and higher relationship to the anti-Semitism of my own homeland.'[2] Ultimately, Herzl's Paris experience was thus a way of understanding not French affairs, but rather the Jewish problem at home, in Vienna. It further gave him the political knowledge, and ambition, to do something about it.

Herzl's experience as a political correspondent was one with which he felt very comfortable. It suited his ability to use every minute of the day usefully, and it compensated for his perceived failure as a playwright, which he admitted to his new correspondent Arthur Schnitzler on several occasions in 1892 and 1893.[3] In March 1893 Herzl wrote to his erstwhile collaborator Hugo Wittmann that all this political journalism was giving him an excellent training in politics. Yet what was the point, unless he entered the political arena. Herzl added: 'But I, a Jew, in Austria?'[4] One of his feuilletons on the Palais Bourbon, however, clearly shows that Herzl had in mind the progression from journalism to political life, at least for other journalists.[5] In early 1894 his new play *Die Glosse* (The Commentary) saw the author attempting, at least in the theatre, to return to the legal profession, if not politics. That he has his legal scholar hero say that his legal interpretation is already 'the sign of a deed' sounds like a Viennese Jewish journalist doing his best to emulate his hero Bismarck, a man not of words but of deeds.[6] Having experienced the excitement of the political world, which comes through his reports despite the veneer of studied disdain, Herzl must have wondered what barred him from taking part. The all too obvious answer for him was that the fact of his Jewishness obstructed his path to political participation.

As we have seen, even before his posting to Paris, the death of Kana had inspired Herzl to sketch a novel on the Jewish question. Over the next five years, until the conversion experience in May 1895, Herzl was to become increasingly obsessed with what to do with the Jews. There is a very long catalogue of incidents which conspired to provoke Herzl to study this question, both in Paris and in Vienna. It is not true that the Dreyfus Affair was the major cause of Herzl's conversion, as legend would have it. The Affair itself actually took place after Herzl's conversion experience, and even the moving spectacle of Dreyfus' degradation in January 1895 was only one of many factors which played a part. Dreyfus, it should be noted, was not mentioned by Herzl in his 1895 diary account of how he came to his idea of the need of the Jews for their own state.[7]

The best way of explaining Herzl's gradual obsession with the Jewish question is to see it as the result of a dialectic between his Viennese experience of anti-Semitism and his perception of Parisian politics and French anti-Semitism. Herzl happened to choose as his home and his place of work the two cities which in the early 1890s had the most active and threatening anti-Semitic movements. In Vienna the lower middle classes were going over en masse to Lueger's anti-Semitic Christian Social Party, and there were various anti-Jewish incidents. In Paris, Drumont had already made his name with La France juive in 1885, and in April 1892, a few months after Herzl had started his new job, Drumont went one step further and started a newspaper, La Libre Parole, which was perhaps one of the most extremely anti-Semitic journals ever published. The appearance of this newspaper led almost immediately to a spate of duels between Jewish army officers and anti-Semites, which led to the death of Captain Mayer in June 1892. Herzl's response to this affair was laden with sarcasm, and expressed his confidence that anti-Semitism was a passing fad in French politics.[8] For a man as concerned with honour as Herzl, however, it must have been most unsettling to see a Jew have to die, because he was a Jew, to defend his honour. That his other close friend, Oswald Boxer, had died while in South America on a mission to find a site suitable for a colony of Jewish refugees from Russia was surely another factor reminding Herzl of the Jewish problem.[9]

He remained acutely aware of the problems, also of the deficiencies and lack of character, of his fellow Jews. In a review of Lavedan's play *Prince Aurec* he criticized the author's portrayal of the Jewish parvenu Baron Horn: 'Horn does not brag enough about his high connections; he doesn't show himself sufficiently honoured, he doesn't stammer with pride and happiness when a Duchess happens to address him. The inner uncertainty of the Jew has not been portrayed in this character. But this uncertainty is the very stamp of the real Horn, in real life; it is his specific characteristic.' It was perhaps necessary for Herzl's own 'self-respect' and self-understanding that he then comments: 'A compassionate understanding realizes, of course, that this insecurity is the fruit of a long, long era of suffering, which has not yet come to an end.'[10]

The irony was that in Paris Herzl could operate without having personally to be affected by anti-Semitism. He was, as he himself later put it, 'unrecognized' in a city where his dark good looks were not exactly uncommon among Frenchmen. That he was 'unrecognized' was something which, he added, showed Austrian and German anti-Semitism to be stupid.[11] For its French counterpart, however, he had more than a touch of admiration. In Paris Herzl attained the status he had long sought: he became an 'exceptional Jew'. That is to say, he gained entrée into the circles of the French literary world, and more than that he became a fairly close acquaintance of writers such as Alphonse Daudet who had strong anti-Semitic sympathies. For them Herzl was not really a Jew; this was the cultural anti-Semitism of Herzl's student days. For much of his career in Paris, with a few exceptions when he doubted that the Third Republic could carry on, Herzl himself felt safe, a neutral observer of the French scene, who could see the 'merits' of anti-Semitism, even 'excuse it'.[12] For was it not true, as Drumont and company said, that the Jews were different, did control a large proportion of French capital and had not assimilated totally into French society; that the Jewish question was above all a modern, social question?[13] If this is indeed what Herzl told Daudet and his fellow dinner guests then it is not surprising that he was an 'acceptable' Jew.

In November 1892, the Panama Scandal, which ranks with the Dreyfus Affair as one of the greatest political crises of the French Third Republic, broke. There was a personal side to the scandal for Herzl, because the central figure was none other than his boyhood hero Ferdinand de Lesseps, the visionary builder of the Suez Canal. His still more visionary and, as it turned out, over-ambitious plan to dig a canal across the Isthmus of Panama had led to his, and very nearly the Third Republic's, undoing. In order to maintain investors' confidence in the project, de Lesseps' company had orchestrated a conspiracy of silence in the French press about the overwhelming difficulties and huge costs of the project. In doing so they had employed the services of two Jewish speculators, Baron de Reinach and Cornelius Herz, who had paid off not only the press but also many deputies to the Palais Bourbon. Eventually, however, the whistle had been blown on the conspiracy, by none other than Edouard Drumont in his *Libre Parole*, which gave the ensuing scandal, involving, it would seem, almost all of the French political establishment, including such upright figures as Georges Clemenceau, an anti-Semitic tinge. The Panama Scandal convinced Herzl, however, not so much of the dangers of anti-Semitism, as of the corrupt and unstable nature of the French political system. That Jewish individuals such as Reinach and Herz were heavily implicated in the scandal can only have increased his 'understanding' of anti-Semitism as a social phenomenon.[14]

Herzl reported on French anti-Semitism. He tried to do something about the Austrian variety. With his new knowledge of modern politics, and his understanding of French anti-Semitism as at base a social protest, Herzl evinced increasing frustration with the Austrian political scene which seemed to be hopelessly behind the times, at least when it came to parliamentary debate. Reporting on a debate in the Reichsrat in 1892 he criticized the unreality of the way it treated the Jewish question as though it had anything to do with religion, when in reality it was a social problem. As he said: 'Today what matters is not the evening meal (Holy Communion) but only one's daily bread.'[15] Having identified it as a social problem, Herzl then suggested to his editors, Moritz Benedikt and Eduard Bacher, his first of many solutions to the Jewish problem. To counter the lower-middle-class threat of anti-Semitism, the *Neue Freie Presse* should publish in their Christmas issue of 1892 a proposal which appears to have been that Jews should threaten to vote for universal suffrage, and thus unleash the forces of socialism, if the Christian Socials persisted in their anti-Semitic campaigning. Bacher and Benedikt replied that they had already thought up a similar approach, but the main opposition to such ideas had come from Jews themselves. Herzl's reply presaged his later Zionist attitude. It was necessary, he opined, to ignore what Jews wanted, and do instead what was best for them. 'For they are a people who have, through oppression, become degenerate and emasculated; confused by money, they are like domesticated animals kept in various pens.'[16] In other words, Jews were hopelessly degenerate, and could no longer find their own salvation. It needed a responsible individual to step in and protect their interests for them. This, as we shall see, was to be precisely Herzl's Zionist rationale.

In December 1892 Herzl was far from Zionism, but he did, in a further letter to Benedikt, have some sort of solution. The only way to counter a movement such as anti-Semitism was through another movement, by which he probably meant socialism. Reflecting his Parisian experience, Herzl states in passing that anti-Semitism is in many respects not a bad thing, because it should have a sobering effect on the flashy rich Jews and amoral Jewish financiers. The problem with it is that it distresses 'better' Jews and makes things difficult for Jews who deserve to come up in the world. This then leads Herzl to consider the option of conversion, to which he, as a 'modern average Jew' and having a completely non-denominational attitude to religion, has no objection. Yet he himself would not convert, because his father is still alive, and he will not abandon the Jews while they are still hated. 'A matter of self-respect.' In any case, he rambles, the case of the Spanish Jews shows that conversion is of no use, and that therefore the 'individual solution' to the Jewish problem is not promising. What is needed is to create an atmosphere of tolerance and then have a mass conversion of all Jews. The only problem is how to create this atmosphere of tolerance, for it cannot, in Herzl's view, be created from above. Here Herzl was obviously thinking very seriously about the Jewish question, but his answers at this stage only create more problems. There was no doubt, however, that something had to be done.[17]

A few weeks later Herzl gave virtually the same reply to Baron Leitenberger, a leading figure in the League for the Defence against Anti-Semitism in Vienna. Anti-Semitism is not all bad; it will create a generation of Jews concerned with honour. Conversion is a sort of solution, and he is considering it for his son. Socialism is the proper answer to anti-Semitism, and the best way Leitenberger can proceed with his plans for a newspaper is to buy a paper from those in the gutter press and use this to smuggle in enlightened and liberal ideas among its readership. The only problem with this is that the paper will then become unpopular, jests Herzl. Not surprisingly, Leitenberger took Herzl to be making fun of him with these facile and 'clever' remarks, and told him so. Herzl replied with a long defence and elaboration of his proposals which reveals much of his state of mind in early 1893.

Herzl denies that his initial reply had only been that of 'a causeur', an accusation to which a supposedly serious German writer such as Herzl would have been particularly sensitive. Reminding Leitenberger that the Jewish question is a 'social' question, he then suggests a two-pronged assault. First, the symptoms of anti-Semitism should be countered by 'brutality'. That is to say 'a half-dozen duels would raise the social position of the Jews considerably.' Secondly, the cause of the evil must be remedied, and Herzl explicitly puts the responsibility for this on the Jews themselves. It is certain 'qualities' of the Jews, for which they are justifiably criticized, with which

the Jews themselves must dispense. Jews must turn the prejudice against them into a pro-Jewish attitude by being
morally better than the rest. This, however, in Herzl's view,
has no hope of success, or at best only for the 'exceptional
Jew'. Having attacked Jewish virtue, Herzl now tries to
redress the balance by stressing how well Jews bear up,
considering the centuries of oppression they experienced, in
'the land of the enemy'. The use of this phrase already
indicates the extent of Herzl's alienation from his
'homeland', but he does not at this stage draw the logical
conclusion. Instead he suggests more assimilation, and repeats
his support for conversion, if not for his generation at least
for the next. His explicit aim in early 1893 is: 'Submergence
into the people!' That this means disappearing into the 'land
of the enemy' does not seem to dawn on him at this
juncture.

Having defended his programme of duels and conversion,
Herzl then repeats his advice that socialism is the only answer
to anti-Semitism, and that Leitenberger and company, well-
meaning though they are, have come along about a decade too
late to remedy matters. Here Herzl shows a fairly accurate
understanding of when anti-Semitism had really got going in
Vienna, for ten years earlier his final split with 'Albia' had
occurred. Even so, a new newspaper might work, if it tries to
cater for popular taste. As a reader, Herzl says, he would
prefer a moderate and fair-minded paper, as Leitenberger is
suggesting. Yet, 'as a politician', he sees that such a newspaper
would be useless because it would not reach the kind of people
that have to be reached. A popular newspaper would have to
be taken over, and its 'opinion' cleaned out. Herzl uses a most
typical metaphor to describe this process of enlightenment: 'In
this way the old drains of a city, through which so much
sewage has flowed, are laid with wires of electric light.' The
technical dreams of Herzl's youth and the political ambitions
of the present were thus combined in the struggle against
anti-Semitism.

The new newspaper, however, would not employ the

journalist Herzl, for he explicitly states that there must be no
Jews of any stripe on the staff, if it is to be a credibly objective
defender of Jews. Herzl the journalist then goes on to give
detailed proposals of what this newspaper should be like,
including much sound advice on it not being as 'boring' as
the usual German Liberal newspaper. The ideal would be a
'liberal–social' paper. It should be written in simple German,
and not hide the evil-doings of Jews. It would help if it had a
section on technological inventions and discoveries. Above all
it has to be cheap. Once Herzl got hold of an idea, his
imagination often got hold of him.[18]

As the Panama Scandal grew ever more sordid, and Vienna
ever more a 'land of the enemy', Herzl's solution to the Jewish
problem coalesced around the twin assault already outlined:
duels and conversion. In his Zionist diary of 1895 he was to
claim that early in 1893 one of his 'dreams' had been to
challenge one of the Viennese anti-Semites, Alois Liechten-
stein, Schönerer or Karl Lueger. He envisaged himself either
having a glorious martyrdom, or, in the manner of Morès in
the Mayer duel, hailing his dead opponent as an honourable
victim, after which he would give a speech at his trial in his
own defence worthy of Lassalle, be acquitted, and then be
offered and decline a seat in parliament.[19]

As for conversion, his Zionist diary also tells us that he
seriously contemplated, and suggested to Bacher and Benedikt, that he make a proposal to the Pope on behalf of the Jews
which would offer the mass conversion of the Jews to
Catholicism in return for the Pope's help against the anti-
Semites. The conversion would take place at noon in St
Stephen's Cathedral in Vienna. The converts would enter the
cathedral with a proud mien, while their leaders, Herzl among
them, would remain this side of the threshold. By not entering
the Promised Land of full integration, Herzl and his fellow
leaders would provide a large degree of sincerity to the
proceedings, and implicitly Herzl would be making himself
·the new Moses. Or perhaps the new Schiller? For he also saw
himself in this sentimental drama as 'releasing to the world this

slogan of racial miscegenation'. It might not be a kiss, but it was after all the modern equivalent.

Herzl was brought down to earth by Moritz Benedikt. 'For hundreds of generations,' he told Herzl, who he must have thought was slightly deranged at this point, 'your race has maintained its Judaism. You now want to be the limit of this development. You cannot, and you must not do this. Anyway, the Pope will never receive you.' In the latter prediction Benedikt was wrong, but he was surely right in his estimate of Herzl's scheme.[20] There are, however, certain elements which are important for understanding Herzl's ultimate solution. There is the fact that Herzl now sees himself in a leadership role. The Mosaic pathos of leading the people to the threshold, but not crossing it oneself, will be often repeated in his thought. One should also note that the centre of the problem, and of the solution, is perceived as being Vienna, not Paris. Perhaps most revealing of all is that he sees the fate of the Jews as being negotiated between himself and the powers that be, by a secret deal, or, as he put it himself, 'a diplomatic peace treaty signed behind closed doors', which a thankful Jewry will then accept after the deal has been made. Herzl was never really a populist.

Out of this dreamland, and back in the role of a political commentator, Herzl continued to see anti-Semitism as for the most part harmless in French politics, as a brief remark in a report on a French electoral meeting suggests.[21] During the summer of 1893 he seems to have been more concerned with introducing the idea of labour assistance to Austria, trying to make what for him appeared the backward politics of that country more in line with the socially advanced politics of France, and at the same time providing himself with a chance to meddle in Austrian politics.[22] The journalist was itching to get involved with the real world.

For much of 1893 Herzl was out of commission due to a protracted illness. He spent much of early 1894 writing his play *Die Glosse*, which, as mentioned above, betokened his renewed interest in law. Meanwhile, according to his later account of 1895, a new idea of the solution to the Jewish problem 'ripened in my mind, in the dark ways of the unconscious'. Moreover, having tried his hand at a political solution to the Jewish question, he now reverted to the status of an observer. He expressed these views at the end of his summer vacation back in Vienna, during a visit to his friend and colleague Ludwig Speidel, Vienna's leading theatre critic.

At this stage Herzl thought he understood anti-Semitism, and no longer saw it as a negative development. He now saw it both as inevitable and as a necessary stage in the solution of the Jewish problem, which was, as before, largely caused by the Jews themselves. They had remained 'foreign bodies' in their host nations. It was not the Jews' fault, but they had, because of their oppression in earlier, less enlightened times, acquired many qualities which were 'socially pernicious'. When they had then been given their legal emancipation, which 'doctrinaire liberals' had thought would make every-one immediately equal, the Jews had continued to act in those antisocial ways which they had acquired previously. Most significantly, they had continued to 'hold on to money' because that was what they had been forced to deal with before emancipation. In other words: 'As we emerged from the ghetto, we were and remained at first ghetto Jews.' They had needed time to adjust, to conform to their new society, but the host peoples had not understood this; neither did they have the patience. They only saw the evils of Jewish existence, and not their historical causes. That the emergent socialist ideas attacked mobile capital made matters worse because Jews were so involved in this side of the economy. When Jews tried to leave the world of money and enter the professions then this was a threat to the opportunities of the native population, which they understandably resisted. Anti-Semitism was thus to a large degree due to the lack of reality of the original rationale of emancipation. 'Actually, anti-Semitism is the consequence of the emancipation of the Jews.'

Yet Herzl viewed this paradoxical conclusion positively, because if anti-Semitism was the product of the emancipation, it might also be the way forward to a true solution. The 'strong and unconscious' anti-Semitism of 'the great crowd' would actually help Jews, because it would be 'the education of a group through the masses, and will perhaps lead to their absorption. One is only educated by severity.' Through this hard school of anti-Semitism, Jews will learn to adapt, in a process of 'Darwinian mimicry', and will become normal human beings again. In an echo of his earlier idea that a movement had to be countered by another movement, Herzl concluded by saying: 'The marks of the former pressure can only be erased by the other pressure.' In other words, anti-Semitism, which he had previously wanted to counter, was now seen as the way to solve the problem of the Jews' otherness. This was the low point of Herzl's attitude to the Jewish question.

After Speidel, Herzl's interlocutor, had laconically described Herzl's ideas as 'world historical', which Herzl erroneously took to be a compliment, his confidence that anti-Semitism would solve itself was severely shaken the same evening by a couple of youths, one in cadet's uniform, who shouted after the carriage in which Herzl was returning to Vienna the simple word 'Saujud' (Jewish pig). This ugly word was bad enough, but what Herzl perceived about it was much worse, and made his ideas on anti-Semitism irrelevant, for he realized that the epithet was not directed against him personally. After all, in Paris he was not treated as a Jew, and how could these two yobs have known who he was? But they did not have to know; as Herzl said, their insult was aimed not at him as a person but at his 'Jewish nose and Jewish beard', at his racial characteristics. Herzl's attempt at theorizing himself out of the Jewish problem, as a social problem, was feeble compared to this simple, religiously derived, but racially motivated slur. As he later wrote: 'When faced with such things, the world historical is useless.'[23]

If simply sitting back and expounding 'tough' theories was as impractical as ideas of mass conversion, what could Herzl do next? His first idea seems to have been to do what he was best at, travel reportage. According to the account in his Zionist diary, he made vague plans to visit all the Jewish communities in the world, including 'the new Zion colonies' (the first mention of the word in his diary) in Palestine. He would show through these reports that the Jews did not deserve their fate, 'that they are human beings, who are criticized without people really knowing about them.'[24] This idea went into abeyance when Herzl returned to Paris. At the beginning of October, in a review of Alexandre Dumas' *La Femme de Claude*, Herzl explicitly rejected one solution to the Jewish question, namely the return to Palestine, as hopeless.[25] Yet it is plain that he was by now deeply involved in trying to do something about this.

On 19 October, while sitting for the sculptor Samuel Friedrich Beer, Herzl became deeply engaged in a conversation about the Jewish question in Austria.[26] As writer and sculptor, the two came to the conclusion 'that it does not help the Jews that they become artists and free of money. The curse remains. We do not escape from the ghetto.' By his own account Herzl then went away, and as if in a dream, just as in an Arab fairytale, he spent the next 17 days in a state of inspiration, writing his latest contribution to the Jewish question. This time, having tried and failed to solve the problem as politician, then world-historical thinker, and travel writer, he went back to his first love, the theatre. Perhaps with the new play, *Das Ghetto* (later *Das neue Ghetto*), Herzl could both achieve lasting fame as a dramatist and set his mind to rest on the Jewish question.

Das neue Ghetto (The New Ghetto) marks Herzl's break with his belief that Jews can be integrated into European society. Its plot is fairly simple. The hero, Jakob Samuel, a Viennese Jewish lawyer (Herzl's former profession), marries a rich Jewish girl who is connected to the Jewish world of Viennese high finance. In order to maintain her in the manner to which she has become accustomed, he allows himself to be sucked into this corrupt world. At the same time he has a pronounced social conscience and sense of honour. He is, after all, a perfectly assimilated Jew. He even has a non-Jewish friend, Franz Wurzlechner, when the play starts. Yet his existence is shown by Herzl to be impossible.

The Jewish milieu of his wife's family results in his Gentile friend, the person who had taught him manners, deserting him—so that he can enter the political world without the albatross of a Jewish friend around his neck. Then the financial machinations of his in-law Rheinberg and a friend of the family, Wasserstein, combined with the social irresponsibility of a Gentile nobleman, von Schramm, conspire to put Samuel in the situation where he cannot, for the sake of his honour, refuse a duel with the Austrian nobleman. This is, in any case, a duel for which he had failed to accept the challenge many years back in his student days. It is doubly impossible to refuse now, 'because I am a Jew'. In the duel Samuel is fatally wounded. His dying words are: 'I want—out! ... Out—out—of—the—ghetto!' The message appears to be that the only way out of the ghetto is through an honourable death.

Das neue Ghetto is a remarkable summary of Herzl's concerns at this time. His hatred of the superficial, materialistic world of Jewish high finance is plain, as is his growing concern for the 'social question', symbolized by the miners, for whom Samuel acts, and whose deaths in a mining disaster bring on the final confrontation with von Schramm. Samuel's description of the way in which Wurzlechner had taught him to behave, and 'overcome' his ghetto self, reveals much about Herzl's former psychological reliance on his 'Christian fellow citizens'. Yet Samuel's insistence that he can now 'go on alone' in his journey away from the ghetto suggests the attempt at self-reliance in the struggle to be 'inwardly free', and thus truly a 'human being' (*Mensch*). Morality, proclaims Samuel, is not the acceptance of one's historically determined condition, rather it is the overcoming of our instinctive nature. The passivity of Wurzlechner and Wasserstein, the Gentile and the Jew, in the face of their backgrounds, is not enough to gain true inner freedom. 'One must go further! Understand?

Further, higher! Only then is one human!'[27] True humanity lies in emancipating oneself from the past.

When Ludwig Speidel saw a performance of the play in 1898, his reaction was to characterize assimilation as the 'second emancipation', and this is indeed a play which sees 'inner freedom' as being identical with breaking down the barriers to one's fellow human beings.[28] It is very much a product of the ideology of emancipation. Yet at the same time it is also describing the tragedy of emancipation, for Samuel's death is symbolic of the impossibility of reconciling the moral imperative of 'inner freedom' and the social reality of Jews and Gentiles. Samuel claims, as Herzl and many liberal and Enlightened emancipationists before him, that the Jews' bad characteristics are not even due to their nature, but rather to their history, and sees their rejection by the Gentiles as unjustified. Yet he also sees that this rejection is only too understandable, as 'Circumstances force people to act the way they do.'[29] Neither side, therefore, can help themselves to be other than they are. Samuel's personal attempt in these circumstances is doomed to tragic failure.

Yet it is clear that the intent should be for the walls of the ghetto to be pulled down. At the core of the play are two dialogues between Samuel and Rabbi Friedheimer. In the first dialogue, the rabbi asks for money to be given to help the poor Russian Jews going overseas to America, and points to how much better off Austrian Jews are, where the walls of the ghetto have come down. Only the visible ones, interjects Samuel. The rabbi replies that anti-Semitism is not so bad, for it increases Jewish piety, and, moreover, 'Our God has rescued us from every Egypt up till now.' Because Jews trusted in God they have survived and kept their old virtues. And their flaws, adds Samuel, to which the rabbi replies that one should not criticize the former life of the ghetto. 'I do not criticize it,' says Samuel. 'I say only that we must get out of it.' The rabbi counters that Jews cannot leave it, and should not leave this 'moral ghetto'. Samuel replies that the Jews must break out of the invisible ghetto, but they must do so from within themselves, free themselves from their own moral limitations.[30] One should be a self-overcomer such as Jakob Samuel.

In the second dialogue, the rabbi warns Samuel against getting too involved in the cause of the workers, that is to say of general humanity. He relates the story of a Jewish boy in the ghetto of fourteenth-century Mainz (the city in which Herzl had heard 'Hep! Hep!') who is lured out of the ghetto by a cry of pain; in attempting to help the apparent sufferer he is murdered. Samuel, asked what this tells him, replies that he is proud of the Jewish boy for answering the cry for help. All Jews must act in the same way, for 'The cry for help can also be real for once.' The rabbi claims that the Jews are too weak to perform this selflessly humanitarian function, but Samuel responds by saying that it is precisely the Jews' weakness which makes their attempt to help general, suffering humanity all the more praiseworthy.[31] In other words, Samuel is left to win the argument in theory, on the moral plane, but loses it in practical, real life. Jews should participate in the outside world, not let themselves be cut off, but in reality their historical and social situation makes it impossible for them to do this. What power the play possesses stems from the fact that there is no resolution, only tension, at its end.

Herzl tried desperately to get this play performed, but he insisted on anonymity.[32] His confidant, and the person through whom he tried to get the play performed, was Arthur Schnitzler. Schnitzler suggested to Herzl that he try and make his portrayal of Jewish life in Vienna less negative, add some more 'sympathetic' characters. Herzl replied that he saw no reason to 'falsify my misanthropy' and averred that 'I absolutely do not want to defend the Jews, or arrange their "rescue". I only want to put the question up for debate, as powerfully as I can.' Herzl's simultaneous perception that he is speaking to a 'people of anti-Semites' shows just how tense his situation had become.[33] In this desperate vision of Vienna, with degenerate Jews on the one hand and an anti-Semitic populace on the other, Herzl was not typical of his generation. By now he had become an atypical, extreme case.

In his refusal to see any 'sympathetic' Jewish types, except his self-image, Herzl went much further in his negative view of Jewishness than Schnitzler, or his near contemporary Sigmund Freud. Neither Schnitzler nor Freud had an uncomplicated relationship with their Jewish identity. Schnitzler was an agnostic, alienated from the outward forms of the Jewish religion, Freud was an atheist. Yet both, in their own ways, had a much more positive image of Jews than the pre-Zionist Herzl. Freud had a sense of Judaism's cultural and ethical contribution to humanity. Schnitzler saw an Enlightened tradition in Judaism; he also wanted Herzl to include some 'strong Jews' in his play. Yet Herzl refused, because for him the Jews were simply a degenerate race, unable to break out of the ghetto, dragging even their best down with them. The thought arises that if Herzl had been better adjusted to his own Jewishness, like his contemporaries Freud and Schnitzler, he might never have felt the need to turn to the Zionist option.

Yet he did, only a few months after completing *Das neue Ghetto*. He says that the play, which was supposed to be a way of writing his way out of the Jewish problem, had the opposite effect: he became more and more involved with the Jewish question and his Jewishness. Why this is so should be clear from the above. The play had no resolution, it left everything hanging in the air. Furthermore, no one would agree to have the play performed, despite Schnitzler's loyal efforts.

Meanwhile the lightning bolt of the trial of Captain Alfred Dreyfus for treason, the ultimate dishonour, had struck in late December, followed by the Jewish 'traitor's' degradation on 5 January 1895, at which the reporter Herzl was famously present. The Dreyfus Affair was to become the most famous of all crises in modern French history, and, in the ultimate vindication of the Jewish captain and the disgrace of the army establishment, was to tilt the balance of French politics decidedly to the Left. The Affair also, ironically, witnessed the apotheosis of French anti-Semitism, and its eventual collapse in the light of the fact that Dreyfus had been framed and that the actual German spy in the French General Staff was another, very non-Jewish figure, with the name of Esterhazy.

It has often been asserted that the Dreyfus Affair was the inspiration for Herzl's Zionism. He himself was later to claim, at the height of the Affair in 1899, that he had known that Dreyfus was innocent, and that it was the trauma of seeing an innocent man being degraded simply because he was Jewish, which made him into a Zionist.[34] Modern scholarship, rightly I think, disputes this claim for two very good reasons. Firstly, the actual Affair did not start until a couple of years after Dreyfus's conviction, and few doubted Dreyfus's guilt at the time of his trial and disgrace. Even among French Jewry, the reaction was one more of shame, and fear of anti-Semitic exploitation of this example of 'Jewish treachery'.[35] Secondly, there is, I repeat, no mention of the Dreyfus trial in Herzl's diary of a few months later where he recounts his 'conversion' to Zionism.

This does not mean, of course, that the trial did not have an impact on Herzl's state of mind at the time. It would certainly have added to the gloom already evident in his Jewish play, and the lesson Herzl might well have gleaned was not so much that Dreyfus was innocent and the French anti-Semites unfairly persecuting him, as that, even if he was innocent, the anti-Semitic response of the French public was understandable given the behaviour of 'certain aggressive Jewish elements' in French society. Furthermore there was the consideration, to which Herzl gave expression in his subsequent diary, that Jews should not be in positions of command in the armies of their hosts, because this caused justified resentment.[36] In other words, the Dreyfus trial was graphic confirmation of the conviction Herzl had already gained that the Jews, because they were indeed a different, separate group, could not integrate successfully into Gentile society, no matter how hard they tried. It is quite possible that Herzl viewed Dreyfus's trial, and the anti-Semitic response to it, not as a case of a persecuted innocent, but rather as proof that a Jew should not be on the French General Staff in the first place. This would actually have been a stronger impulse to his Zionism than the reason he later gave. Whatever the impact on Herzl, one thing is clear: the Dreyfus trial was not the blinding revelation which alone turned him into a Zionist. It was only one of many factors making him wonder about the place of Jews in Western society.

He went for the first time to a synagogue in Paris, and 'looked at the Jews present there; I saw the family resemblance of their faces. Bold, misshapen noses, shy and cunning eyes.' He now saw for himself the physical resemblance of which he had been reminded in Austria. Indeed it was while on a brief visit back to Austria, at the end of March and beginning of April, that Herzl experienced the final straw in the long process which had taken him from unconcerned, journalistic dilettante to a man obsessed with the idea that 'I had to do something for the Jews.' On 1 April, an eminently suitable date, Karl Lueger's Christian Socials won an electoral victory in the Second Curia which spelled the beginning of the end of the liberal hegemony in Viennese politics. With the lower middle classes behind him, now joined by vast swathes of the middle classes of teachers and officials, Lueger appeared on the brink of becoming the first elected anti-Semitic mayor in any European capital. It was the death knell of liberal politics not only in Vienna, but in Austria generally. It was with this crushing realization, that anti-Semitism was not only an annoying minority movement as it was in French politics, but was now the major political force in his own home city, that Herzl returned to Paris in a state of great agitation.

He seems first to have considered reviving his plans for a travel reportage on the world's Jewish communities. Then, some time before Easter (14 April), he discussed the Jewish question with his friend Alphonse Daudet. Daudet confessed himself an anti-Semite; Herzl in turn started expounding his new views on the question, and got fairly carried away, as was his wont. On hearing that Herzl wanted to write a book 'for and about the Jews', Daudet asked if he intended to write a novel. No, came the reply, 'rather a book for men!' Daudet suggested, giving the emancipatory example of *Uncle Tom's Cabin*, that a novel would have greater impact. Herzl 'speechified further' and, having enthused Daudet and himself with his ideas, he then took Daudet's advice and went back to his *Samuel Kohn* novel about Kana. Instead of ending with a triumphant and reconciling suicide as in the original version (and, very nearly, in *Das neue Ghetto*), now the hero was no longer Kohn/Kana, but rather his friend (Herzl), who, by life's good fortune, manages 'to discover the Promised Land, or rather found it'. About to set sail on his voyage thither, he receives Kohn's suicide note, and in his anger exclaims: 'A lost life, which belonged to us!' Herzl had thus solved the problem of his protagonist by substituting his own mode of solving problems, escape through travel. He had run away many times from his responsibilities as a husband; he had thought of 'travelling' as an answer to the Jewish question, by reporting on Jews. Now, finally he went one stage further, and had his hero (himself) travel overseas to an unknown land.

The plan for the novel became converted into a practical proposal, in an 'unconscious' process, which probably had something to do with Herzl finally wanting to write a 'book for men', that is to say, to be taken seriously as a writer and politician. At the end of April he wrote a letter to Baron de Hirsch, the well-known Jewish banker-philanthropist, and two weeks later summoned up the courage to mail it. This eventually led to an interview with the baron on Whitsunday, 2 June; this day marks the start of Herzl's Zionism.[37]

What had Herzl realized now that set him on his Zionist path? Part of the answer may be that he had seen that the tensions of the 'new ghetto' could never be resolved here, in Europe. The tension between the aim of participating fully in the fate of humanity and the reality of anti-Semitism certainly had not been resolved in his play. Instead the 'inner dialectic' of the situation appeared to necessitate that the problem become an international one, be externalized, projected abroad. If Jews were ever to break down the invisible walls of the ghetto, external and internal, the only way to achieve this was to do it somewhere else, where the pressures of anti-Semitism and history did not prevail. Internal liberation could only come from external migration. With this, the insight of a man who had never really settled down anywhere, Herzl proceeded to expound his 'solution' to the Jewish problem.

3
THE STATE OF THE JEWS

On 16 June 1895 Herzl wrote a letter to Rabbi Güdemann of Vienna, asking him to help in his new quest. Herzl hoped that the rabbi would come to his aid, but, even if that help was not forthcoming, he would press ahead, 'for I have found the solution to the Jewish question.'[1] It was to be several months before *Der Judenstaat: Versuch einer modernen Lösung der Juden-frage* was published.* Yet this publication was only the latest version of an idea which Herzl had had back in May 1895, and which he had been trying to persuade the élite of world Jewry to accept ever since. Only when the world of high finance rebuffed him did the élitist Herzl decide that his plans, with some of the more aristocratic features removed, should be made known to the public. The publication of *Der Judenstaat* set the seal on the transformation of what had started as an attempt at a 'behind closed doors' solution to the Jewish question, imposed from above, into the mass movement of political Zionism.

Der Judenstaat is what made Herzl into the father of the state

---

* *Der Judenstaat* is usually translated as *The Jewish State*, but this is not fully accurate. The proper translation should be *The Jews' State*, or, perhaps better, *The State of the Jews*. This conveys much better Herzl's intentions than the more ethnically oriented 'Jewish state'. Herzl explicitly rejected a 'Hebrew state' in favour of his 'Juden-staat', state of Jews, 'where no one has to be ashamed that he is a Jew' (see below, p. 40). The translation of the full title should thus be: *The State of the Jews: an attempt at a modern solution to the Jewish question.*

of Israel. It is the central justification for regarding him as a 'Jewish thinker', for, more than any other single work, it provided Zionism, and thus to a large extent modern Jewish identity, with its dominant rationale. In its realization that the Jews were 'a people. One people', and that this people needed, indeed the whole world needed, a state of the Jews, where Jews could be Jews, this book forcefully underpinned the new sense of Jewish nationality which was emerging, and did so much more effectively, and much more famously, than any previous attempt on these lines. Herzl may not have been original in his thought (although his ignorance of previous works meant that for him it was original), but his position as a famous Viennese journalist, combined with the cogency of his arguments, meant that this document was really the crucial one in the history of Zionist thought. Without *Der Judenstaat* there might never have been a state of Israel.

There is a surprising amount of continuity between the slightly pathological attitude of the pre-Zionist Herzl to the Jews, and the Herzl who proudly proclaimed his membership of the Jewish people. While the book is plainly an identification with the Jewish people, and the suggestion of a practical way of rescuing them from their dangerous situation among anti-Semitic societies, it is also a book intended to show how Jews can be reformed, how they can be made fit for statehood. Most importantly, it is a book concerned with honour, with self-respect, and with 'inner freedom'. In other words, the 'modern solution to the Jewish question' turns out to be that Jews can only become whole human beings, truly free, and able to contribute to the well-being of Mankind, when they are among themselves, possessed of their own, sovereign state. The only real Jewish emancipation, as Herzl himself wrote, is a national, independent state.[2] The state of the Jews is therefore not only a practical refuge for the Jewish masses, it is the way of resolving the conflict identified in *The New Ghetto*, between the moral imperative of 'leaving the ghetto', of fully joining with Mankind and thus fulfilling the promise of emancipation, and the fact of the historically determined separation of Jews from their host nations. Herzl's dialectical solution is that, precisely through a radical, geographical separation of the Jews from the other nations, a proper relation, and hence union, with the rest of the world can be effected. By uniting in a Jewish nation, Jews can shake off those negative qualities which Herzl had so despised, and which for him had marked the failure of emancipation. The state of the Jews is thus not only an attempt to liberate the Jews from external oppression, it is also an attempt to break down the internal obstacles, the invisible walls of the 'new ghetto' which had prevented Jews from being morally proper, self-respecting human beings. The state of the Jews not only makes Jews free, it also makes them better.

There are at least four extant versions of the idea which forms the basis of *Der Judenstaat*. There is the original set of notes that Herzl wrote for his initial meeting with Hirsch, which is surprisingly full, and 22 pages long. Then there are the copious notes in his diary for 'The Jewish cause', whose date of commencement is given by Herzl as Whitsun 1895, a remarkable date for beginning the diary of the Zionist movement. These jottings were written on anything available during Herzl's near-manic episode after the meeting with Hirsch, when Herzl was completely obsessed with his 'mighty dream'. This collection of inchoate ideas was then put together by Herzl in a fleshed-out version of his Hirsch notes to produce the third extant, and the first elaborated version, which is his 68-page 'Speech to the Rothschilds', written within two weeks of the Hirsch meeting. This, with some variations and additions, became *Der Judenstaat*, of 86 printed pages, published on 14 February 1896. (The book itself was preceded by an English summary of the book's central ideas in *The Jewish Chronicle* of 17 January.)

Each version is interesting in itself for what it tells us of Herzl's state of mind during this time, as well as the development of his thought. The first version, the notes for the Hirsch meeting, are remarkable for showing the extent to which Herzl had already worked out his ideas, indeed much of his future political strategy, before the famous period of inspiration which followed that meeting on Whit Sunday.[3] It also shows how much Herzl's previous ideas flowed into the new mould he had discovered. There are three leading ideas. First, the main problem with the Jews is that they do not have a united leadership. Second, the 'national character' of the Jews has to be improved in Europe. Third, the best solution to the Jewish problem is to 'create a movement' (literally) to form a new state, a new 'Promised Land', where Jews can rule themselves.

In criticizing the lack of central leadership among Jews, Herzl dismisses attempts to alleviate the plight of poor Jews through charity and colonies in Argentina. This is useless, only creating a class of beggars. 'Never forget,' he remarks, 'spoiled race.' Hirsch is wasting his money. Colonization in some form is a good idea, but first Herzl suggests the 'improvement' of the race here in Europe, making them 'fighting fit, eager to work and virtuous', qualities which in German resonate with Herzl's former German nationalist allegiances. This 'improvement' can start now, to prepare for the exodus from 'Egypt' which will occur in 40 years' time. The former Exodus will become, in its simplicity, a symbol for its modern successor.

Herzl sees the main tactic of improvement as not directly 'buying' Jews, as Hirsch had attempted through his philanthropy, but rather the indirect policy of instituting prizes for various achievements by Jews, which can then be publicized and improve the image, and self-image, of Jews. Among these prizes is one, typically, for the invention of an aircraft. Other prizes reveal more aspects to Herzl's wishes at this juncture. If the Jews are to stay in Europe, then prizes should be given to Jews who fight against each other as members of their respective armies. Herzl cites Kadimah, the Jewish duelling fraternity in Vienna, as a model of how to create true honour among Jews. The state, Herzl then argues, maintains itself by its direction and rewarding of murder, that is to say its honouring of its military heroes. The secret of statecraft is to govern through exploiting the 'imponderable' aspects of men, their pride and their love of their children; hence honours and inherited nobility. Until now, on the other hand, Jews have known nothing of this military approach: they 'were raised to be leeches', and the Jewish spirit is too 'cynically degenerate' to appreciate the power of the state's system of honour. Hence the need for these prizes for virtue. Furthermore, if Jews are to stay in Europe, there should also be prizes for mixed marriages, where the children would be brought up in the majority faith. This is Herzl's 'proper Pope idea' and should be carried out with the agreement of the Pope, the Russian minister Pobedonostsev, and the German Emperor Wilhelm II. The solution of the Jewish problem in Europe remains what Herzl had suggested back in 1893, the complete disappearance of Jews into their host nations.[4]

The preferred alternative, however, is now emigration, if Jews want to become 'human beings' within the next forty years. Herzl already knew at this point the bare bones of how he wanted to organize this new exodus. A congress of notables would be called, in this instance by Hirsch, which would include representatives from all Jewish communities. These people would be faced with their misery, their base condition, and shown the future vision of the 'Promised Land'. They would then be persuaded to make the 'Jewish Association', by which Herzl probably means the Jewish Colonial Association, into the 'impersonal Moses', or, as described elsewhere, 'the Moses travel agency'.

Herzl then puts into Hirsch's proposed speech a great many of the ideas which later appear in *Der Judenstaat*. The Jews are 'pariahs', who are not allowed any honourable career, and are forced into the money world or blamed for socialism. The only way out is the Promised Land, which Jews can create for themselves. 'We are going to build a new world.' It might be in Argentina; as Moses did, the Jews will send out an exploratory expedition. The new land will have hydro-electric power, and the cities, based on Paris, Rome, Florence and Genoa, will utilize all modern inventions. Indeed the emigration will take the form of whole communities transferring en bloc, bringing with them their old customs and habits, and finding their old homeland again in the new land, only in a better form. There will be no one language, certainly not Hebrew, but rather a federal linguistic structure. The state will not be 'a Hebrew state', but rather 'a state of Jews, where no one has to be ashamed that they are a Jew.'

The Jewish Association, which will have the legal status of an English subject, will organize everything, including the liquidation of Jewish assets in Europe, and the building of 'houses that are castles' for the poor in the Promised Land. The economy will be built by the unleashing of the Jewish entrepreneurial spirit. Meanwhile the cultural side will not be neglected, and museums, theatres, music-halls will be built, along with universities and government buildings. The rich will also build their palaces anew. All this construction of a new state will give 'our intellectual proletariat', a group which Herzl elsewhere describes as 'my kind, in a word',[5] the chance of gainful employment, which will immediately reduce the pressure on professional jobs in Europe, one of the main causes of anti-Semitism. All this development of the Promised Land, Herzl is careful to add, will take place under 'strict discipline from the start, for we are a wretched people, and must bring ourselves up.'

Herzl then proceeds to consider how to negotiate with the great powers over this emigration. His first thought is Emperor Wilhelm II, followed immediately by the idea of a state of the Jews under English sovereignty. Yet it is the German emperor who occupies his mind most at this stage. He imagines a personal interview with Wilhelm at which he explains the Jewish problem to the Kaiser. Here Herzl rehearses all the arguments we have already seen, that the Jews are a social menace despite themselves in that 'money owns us' (not the other way round), that the Jews cannot be made into farmers because the German farmers would not allow it, and that this leads to an overly large middle class where Jews compete for too few jobs with Germans. As confiscation of

Jewish capital would only lead to state bankruptcy and a socialist revolution, that is not an option. (Jews have kept their wealth in mobile capital.) Without Jews, on the other hand, Germany will remain great, and be loved by Jews. For, ironically, 'we have become nationally Germans—Yid German!—and will remain so, even on the other side of the ocean.'[6]

In a Germany without Jews everything will be cheaper, and there will be less competition. The loss of a few thousand soldiers will be easily made good, and in any case Jews make bad soldiers, because they are not given any honour. The reason for this is that Jews cannot be made generals, and rightly so, for the anti-Semitic people cannot be expected to serve under Jewish leaders. After this, which appears to be Herzl's first, very ambivalent response to the Dreyfus verdict (repeated in the diary and the Rothschild speech, but radically modified in *Der Judenstaat*),[7] Herzl then goes on to say that it is too late for the emperor to speak for the Jews, remaining neutral would allow the fire of anti-Semitism to burn further, and opposing the Jews would just make the Jews into socialists, or special laws against Jews would force Jews to the Promised Land in any case. The best thing would be for the emperor to be 'the good pharaoh', who would go down in history as the man who had redeemed the Jews, 'who,' added Herzl in parenthesis, 'cannot anymore be burnt to death.'

After this conclusion to his interview with the emperor, Herzl then considers what will happen if the majority at the congress (of notables) does not go along with his plans. The answer is simple: he will go ahead with the minority, and if necessary alone, so convinced is he of his mission. The movement will be created by the simple slogan of going home. Dreams created the German Reich, and they can create the Promised Land for the Jews. The masses can be appealed to, and they can be made to support the cause. For Herzl understands the crowd, and realizes, as he illustrates by his explanations of why crowds gather at Longchamps race day and at the market place, that only through 'vague promises' can men be led, only through hope. The movement will grow to be like Lourdes, and will become 'one of the greatest machines'. Everyone will eventually be caught up in it, even the late-comers, who will be given less honour. The original pioneers will become the nobility, but everyone will have 'honour, freedom, fatherland'.[8]

I have discussed Herzl's original version in some detail, because it shows how well developed Herzl's ideas were from the very start, and how close they were to his previous positions. That honour and fatherland should be two of the main things gained in the Promised Land, and that Jews would remain 'nationally German' there, as well as his analysis of why Jews have to leave, all show the effect of his former German nationalism. That the Promised Land is at one and the same time a land where Jews can be Jews without shame, and live their accustomed lives but in better conditions, and be reformed, also reflects his former negative image of Jews and the ambivalence of his emancipatory purpose. It should further be noted that in this version the division between total assimilation in Europe, and Jewish identity in the state of the Jews, is made quite clear in a way it is not in subsequent drafts. There is no doubt, however, that Herzl now sees that if Jews want to be true 'human beings', that is to say truly emanci-pated, they must form their own state. He is also clear, at this early stage, that this must be done through a congress and a Jewish Association, and through negotiations with the great powers. If only Hirsch had listened to Herzl's whole speech, he would have heard the basic strategy of *Der Judenstaat* six months before it was published.

With his basic ideas already formulated, Herzl could now afford to have another of his attacks of inspiration. The second version, the collection of scattered notes, was the result of this manic period, when, famously, performances of Wagner's *Tannhäuser* were Herzl's main form of distraction, and an apparent source of inspiration.[9] They provide a fascinating insight into Herzl's state of mind, for they were written without his own internal censorship, so that his imagination should not be limited.[10] There are several points in these notes, therefore, when the reader can but cringe at what Herzl has written. One of the worst instances is yet another attempt to express the negative effects of Jewish existence in Western society: 'We have indeed become a scourge for the peoples who once tortured us. The sins of their fathers revenge themselves on them. Europe is now being punished for the ghettos. It is true that we suffer from the suffering we cause. It is a scourge of scorpions, that is to say living scorpions, who cannot be held guilty for the fact that they did not become lions, tigers or sheep. The scorpions receive after all the worst martyrdom from the scourging.'[11] Here Herzl comes perilously close to calling Jews vermin.

Yet the point is that his plan will redeem the Jews from their awful fate. At one point in his diary he describes himself as 'the man who makes aniline from refuse'.[12] What he means by this, as a short story of his, 'The Aniline Inn', clearly demonstrates, is not so much that Jews are 'refuse' to be transformed, as that they are the most desperate part of humanity, who, with his redemptive plan, can be made to embrace life fully again, and regain their self-respect.[13] This is also the symbolic message of Herzl's vision of the coronation ceremony for the 'Doge' of the new Jewish 'aristocratic republic', where the doge will enter wearing the 'costume of shame' of a medieval Jew, with yellow badge and pointed hat, and only on having been crowned will he come forth wrapped in the cloak of respectability.[14]

Above all, Jews in the new state will be honourable once more. A theme repeated many times in these notes is the one of Jewish honour. The original settlers are envisaged, in another of Herzl's dramatic flights of fancy, as becoming 'the knights of Jewish honour', complete with their yellow ribands, the Jewish version of the legion of honour. At another point Herzl looks forward to the vanity of Jewish snobs being superseded by ambition, the search for honour. Herzl is so intent on rescuing Jewish honour that he is prepared to put the business of the liquidation of Jewish assets in the hands of the anti-Semites, to ensure that none think that the Jews are, even in their departure, trying to exploit others unfairly. Herzl repeatedly states that his plan is a solution, because it makes of the Jews' enemies their friends. Everyone is satisfied, and so 'Jewish honour begins'.[15]

What is more, Jews in the new state will be forced to learn the 'duties of freedom'. At times Herzl has his doubts whether the 'ghetto natures' of his Viennese Jewish acquaintances, who have become used to the 'comfort of captivity', will understand the 'call to freedom and becoming human'; he also employs at one point the image of 'a wall, which is the degeneracy of the Jews', which he cannot break down, but on the other side of which he can see 'freedom and greatness'. For most of the time he is confident that his new state will provide the inner freedom the Jews so desperately need. He bases this confidence on the realization that the Promised Land 'is within ourselves', that it is up to Jews and within their power to achieve this dream, and also on his perception that the state of the Jews is a 'world necessity', because it solves the Jewish question for Jew and Gentile alike.[16]

Indeed, Herzl comes to see in the course of these notes that the solution to the Jewish question, the state of the Jews, is also the solution to the social question, because it offers an opportunity to realize progressive social ideas, such as the system of labour assistance, the seven-hour day and garden cities, on virgin soil, without the drag of history. Jews such as his father were forced by circumstance to be brokers, but that was in the past. Now society can be organized without such soul-destroying careers.[17] Herzl, although he promises to protect the rights of the individual, likens his plans to a kind of state socialism, of which he approves, as long as it intends 'the gradual rise of all to the distant, high goals of humanity'. In thus providing a 'model state' for the whole world, the Jews will be making a major contribution to the general well-being of Mankind. 'But if that were true, what a gift of God to the Jews!' exclaims Herzl.[18] The state of the Jews has become in his eyes a sort of Jewish mission, based on the ideology of emancipation. The emancipation of the Jews was originally the product of Western tolerance, which could not be realized there, in Europe. Yet this precious gift of tolerance has been given to the Jews. Now the main Jewish characteristics will be 'freedom and relief', and their new state will have complete religious freedom, as well as being the most socially advanced state in the world. It will thus be able to pay back the gift of tolerance by being in the vanguard of human liberation. No wonder the state of the Jews is a world necessity, in Herzl's eyes.[19]

As well as these central themes, many of the notes are elaborations of ideas already present in the Hirsch speech, such as the stress put on the 'imponderables' in politics, and on the need to transfer people's environment from the old to the new world, also Herzl's assessment of the language question. The 'inspired' Herzl also adds many touches of detail, some practical, some bizarre, as regards, among other topics, ceremonial, culture, technology, the economy, and the social and constitutional organization of the state. In discussions of the latter his contempt for democratic politics is very evident, as is his wish for some sort of meritocratic aristocracy. His élitist attitude is also clear in his statement that he will work for the Jews, not with them, a stance which is reflected in the theoretical backing which he provides to his campaign, and which eventually appears in Der Judenstaat. In these pages he further discusses his strategy: find a suitable land, sign a treaty with its present sovereign, gain a diplomatic guarantee from the great powers, and then issue a Jewish loan. He contemplates the future foreign policy of the new state towards its probably South American neighbours. Of one thing he is sure, the new state will not have any plans to invade its neighbours: 'New Judea should only rule through the spirit.'[20]

Herzl assimilated most of these ideas into the 'Speech to the Rothschilds', the third version of his plan, written only a couple of weeks after the notes for the Hirsch interview.[21] Already, Herzl is concerned almost exclusively with the exodus 'from Mizraim'. This Rothschild speech is, indeed, so similar to *Der Judenstaat*, that only the major points where the two differ need be discussed here. At this stage, for instance, he still favours Argentina over Palestine, for the attraction of the legend of the old Promised Land does not overcome its impracticality for Herzl's 'system of transplantation'. Speaking to a still private audience, Herzl also allows himself a larger latitude of confidentiality than in his published work. Thus he is more open about the evils of the Jews being 'a people of stockbrokers', and the dangers inherent in the Rothschilds' financial power, which even they cannot control, he claims. In the Promised Land there will be a stock exchange state monopoly to prevent Jews becoming jobbers again. He jocularly remarks that the other nations will also have to impose such state ownership on their stock exchanges, if they do not want their societies to be 'jewified'.[22]

In consideration of his audience, Herzl stresses what for him is the inevitability of social revolution in France, which will confiscate all Jewish wealth there. On Austria, too, he is more open than in the published version: 'In Austria the government will allow itself to be cowed by the Viennese crowd into handing over the Jews. In Austria the mob can achieve anything it desires. Only the mob does not know this yet. Its leaders will soon teach it, though.'[23]

He is also somewhat more explicit about the kind of constitution he wants. The state will be an 'elective principality', but with the prince having his powers strictly controlled by the constitution; 'for we will be free men, and have no one above us but almighty God.' Herzl then repeats his elaborate coronation scene, only to wonder whether his audience thinks he is relating a novel to them. Although he justifies festive occasions as not masquerades, but rather 'deeply meaningful memorials of the past', it is notable that he dropped this coronation scene from the final version of *Der Judenstaat*. Further to his image of the new state, he argues against democracy, citing Swiss legislation against Jews, stresses that politics must come from above, and predicts that German will be the state's official language.

In his concluding remarks Herzl adds what could be seen as a personally revealing comment on his plan. There is no doubt that the new state will be the 'Promised Land', Herzl asserts, for it will be the land 'where we will not be automatically despised for having crooked noses, red or black beards and bow legs'.[24] The nose and beard which had identified Herzl as a Jew in the Austrian countryside are no longer an issue, over there. This passage was cut from the published version.

Between the 'Speech to the Rothschilds' and the publication of *Der Judenstaat* several months elapsed. During this period Herzl tried to get Bismarck, his great hero, to support him, but his letter went unanswered. Nor did the Rothschilds or the world of Jewish high finance rally to his colours. Herzl thus decided to go public. In the interim there were more elaborations of his ideas in his diary, but when it came to publication he left out many of the more fanciful notions which had entered his mind since the beginning of June. The time to dream was now over; with *Der Judenstaat*, Herzl wrote the 'book for men' which he had aimed to do at the start.

Der Judenstaat, Herzl's fourth version of his plan, is, as will have become evident, the end product of a complex process, stretching back long before Herzl's 'conversion' in May and June 1895. It thus rehearses arguments which will have become familiar. It is also important to realize that it is Herzl's public version of his plan, a political pamphlet in effect, and cast very much as a plan of action. Much has been made of Herzl's belief in the power of dreams, and this was certainly a strong part of his character, albeit in the sense described earlier. Yet *Der Judenstaat* is a dream to be realized, to be made real. As he had written to Hirsch back in June, 'the fantasies of the people must be given a firm ground.'[25] It is presented very much as a practical proposal. It is precisely not a 'dream state', as Herzl calls the *Freiland* of Theodor Hertzka, another Hungarian Jewish Viennese journalist. Instead the slogan of the book is 'No fairytale, no delusion'.[26] It is on its practicality that Herzl bases the value of his plan.

This is also the theme with which he starts his book. 'I

47

invent nothing' are virtually the author's first words in the foreword. His plan is not a 'fantasy', but at most a 'combination' of ideas and resources which are already present in the world. It is not a utopia, but eminently realizable. This is because it is not a complicated machine with no motivating power, such as Hertzka's construction. Herzl's machine is designed to answer a specific need, the need of the Jews, which will provide more than enough 'motive power' to propel his machine forward. As he says, using a typical technological metaphor, this need has already produced 'tea kettle phenomena' such as the Zionist experiments in Palestine. That pressure just needs to be put to good use. This is what his plan is designed to do.[27]

Having asserted the practicality of his plan, Herzl then claims inevitability for its realization: 'the state of the Jews is a world necessity, therefore it will arise.' At the same time he calls for the 'best' Jews to rally round, for an individual cannot realize this plan on his own, but must have mass support. Indeed he wonders if he is not ahead of his time, and whether his plan will only be realized by a better, future generation, when 'the Jews who will it shall have their state, and will have deserved it.'[28] In claiming that history is with him, and yet on the other hand relying on the power of the will, Herzl, as Arthur Hertzberg has acutely pointed out, manages to combine the two poles of nineteenth-century thought, Marx and Nietzsche.[29] Then again this faith in the future was perhaps necessary considering that the Jewish establishment had by this time rebuffed his ideas. How else could Herzl realize 'the higher pride and the happiness of inner freedom in one's being' which came just by starting the campaign for a state of the Jews?

In the introduction which follows Herzl emphasizes that technological progress has provided us with the means to solve the problems of humanity, including the Jewish question. That the Jewish question exists is clear for Herzl. Anti-Semitism exists wherever Jews are. Where it does not yet exist, such as England, Jews fleeing from persecution will bring it with them, as has happened in America. Anti-Semitism occurs despite the good intentions of the civilized nations, because it is a survival of the Middle Ages which cannot be shaken off. Mankind does progress, but only terribly slowly, and not fast enough for any quick solution to the Jewish question—in Europe.

Herzl claims to understand anti-Semitism. A great deal of it is superstition, envy and prejudice, but part of it at least is a genuine sense of the need for self-defence. For Herzl now realizes that the Jewish question is not a religious question, but nor is it a social question. Instead it is a 'national question' which needs to be considered as a 'political world question' which has to be regulated by the international community. The core of Herzl's argument is that 'We are a people, *one* people.' He might just as well have stressed the word 'people', for what Herzl has done is taken the Jew from society, and put him on the world stage. This is the externalization of the internal dialectic of *Das neue Ghetto*.

Jews have everywhere tried to assimilate, 'to submerge themselves', in their host societies, only keeping the faith of their fathers, but have never been regarded as anything but 'strangers'. This is because the peoples of Europe are endemically anti-Semitic; even 'the fairytale and the proverb are anti-Semitic'. Mixed marriage would be the only true assimilation, but this is a strategy which only the rich can pursue. It cannot, Herzl argues, be a general solution. Then again, it is not a desirable solution in any case, because the 'personality' of the Jewish people cannot and should not disappear. Those Jews who want to fall away from the tree and assimilate can continue to do so, with greater ease if the real Jews leave for their new land. Yet the Jews must survive by moving to this new state.

That they can be moved is something Herzl does not doubt. Previous attempts at Jewish colonies have failed because they did not have a proper goal. Herzl has now provided this goal with his 'state idea', which is nothing else but 'the royal dream' which the Jews have never ceased dreaming. All that needs to be done is to show that 'a thought as clear as day can be made of this dream.' Herzl promises that the new state will be just as civilized as the states the Jews presently inhabit, indeed it will be better. Meanwhile the start of the exodus will bring relief to the Christian populace in Europe, who can look forward to a society without Jews. The Jews will thus part as friends, and when back in Europe can now be honest as real foreigners, citizens of another state, the state of the Jews.[30]

There follows a 'General section' in which Herzl recapitulates his theory of anti-Semitism, and the need for a state of the Jews. In his view equal rights for Jews have been *de facto* rescinded; Jews are denied jobs in the higher echelons of the military and civil service. There are economic boycotts. All over Europe, from Russia to France, Jews are badly off. The rich are uncomfortable, the middle classes depressed, the poor desperate. The pressure is 'Jews out!' and things will not get better, for all the peoples of Europe are anti-Semitic. They do not have the historical consciousness to realize that the Jewish 'threat' is due to the fact that 'We are what the ghettos made us.' Jews were forced into the world of money, as they are now forced to enter the stock exchange, for want of a more honourable career. At the same time the Jews are producing a host of 'intellectuals of middling calibre' who have no suitable career options and will thus find themselves on the side of socialism. The 'social battle' which threatens will thus hurt the Jews the most, because they will be the most exposed group among both the capitalists and the socialists. Previous solutions, such as turning Jews into farmers, are misguided, as there is no point in trying to turn back the clock of history. In any case the peasants would never allow it. Assimilation, as has been shown, is no solution.

The real cause of anti-Semitism is the emancipation of the Jews itself. Jews were no longer 'fit for emancipation' when the legal emancipation was instituted, for by then the Jews had become a 'middle-class people' which offered too strong a competition for the Christian middle class, and which therefore faced pressure from within the bourgeoisie (from the

Christians), and from without (the working class). Here Herzl has markedly shifted his ground, from claiming that the ghetto produced moral degeneracy to saying that the problem with the ghetto was that it made the Jews into a too successful bourgeois group. This is just one of the instances where Herzl's public voice is more favourable about Jews than his private views would indicate. Whatever the interpretation of the effects of the ghetto, Herzl remains convinced that one thing is certain: the emancipation, once granted, cannot be rescinded. All Jews would in that case become revolutionaries, and even the attempt to seize Jewish wealth would only boomerang, because Jewish wealth is in mobile capital, and any attack on this would hurt the whole economy. The fact that one cannot, therefore, overcome the Jews only increases the hatred of them.

Herzl then sums up his views by stating that the long-term cause of anti-Semitism is the loss during the Middle Ages of the ability of the Jews to assimilate, and that the short-term cause is the over-production of middling intellectuals, who have no 'healthy' way up or down, and thus Jews come to control the 'money power' and at the same time provide the officers of the revolution.

He claims there is no hope of breaking the spiral of hatred in Europe, and repeats his view that assimilation is impossible and in any case not to be wished. The personality of the Jewish people is 'too famous and despite all degradations too elev-ated' for us to want it to disappear. And Jews band together precisely when they are under the most pressure. This brings Herzl to his basic definition of Jewish identity: 'Thus we are and remain, whether we like it or not, a historical group which recognizably belongs together. We are a people—the enemy makes us one without our having any say in the matter.' The irony is that, once forced by the enemy back on their Jewish identity, Jews then prove themselves strong enough to form a 'model state'.

All that is necessary is sovereignty over a piece of land; the Jews' moral and legal persons, the Society of Jews and the

Jewish Company, will look after the rest and build a modern state which will look forward and not back. From this point, having justified his new state, Herzl can indulge his interest in detailed planning. He discusses whether Palestine or Argentina is a more suitable goal, and the fact that he discusses Palestine in much more detail reveals the effect of his first meetings with other Zionists. He envisages at this stage, by the way, that a state of the Jews in Palestine will be a bastion of European culture against Asian barbarity, and further that the Holy Places will be given an extra-territorial status, with a Jewish guard of honour, another symbol of the reconciliation of history. Then there is a brief philippic against 'practical' people who do not believe his plan will succeed, in which Herzl uses the case of the railways to show that enough imagination and enough incentive can create markets, and economies. His, in other words, is a dynamic solution.[31]

This leads to the more detailed sections of the book, in which Herzl first discusses the *modus operandi* of his proposed legal person, the Jewish Company, how it will go about transferring people and resources to the new state, and ensure that this new society, with its garden cities, seven-hour day and so forth, will be a model of progress. He discusses the way it will raise money, from the rich Jews, and if not them, from the middling Jewish bankers, and if not from them, then from a popular subscription, a kind of referendum as he calls it. After this he has a section on the 'communities' in which he describes his plans of transferring whole communities intact, so that they feel 'at home' in the new land. Indeed it will be better than home because in improved conditions. The communities will be led by a rabbi, as is only correct, considering that Jews are historically a group bound together by religion, not language (the second definition Herzl provides of Jewish identity). Herzl uses the description of the forms of emigration to expound on his theory of the crowd, which he sees as driven by incentive and by hope, in this case the hope of a land finally free of anti-Semitism, 'the free homeland'. He then states that the first who emigrate will get the best pieces of land, thus providing the most concrete incentive of all.[32]

There follows a section on the relation of the state of the Jews to its originator, the Society of Jews, the moral person of Herzl's plan. Herzl reminds us that the creation of a new state is not all that unusual. He cites the way colonies are becoming independent states, vassal states are breaking away, and new territories have become free states (as in the USA). The state of the Jews is different from these in that it has no territory as yet, but neither has the Pope, and what is important is not so much the land but the fact of a group of people bound together by a sovereign authority. Herzl's problem is how to give his movement, his Society of Jews, the authority of a sovereign state. His solution is the theoretical backbone of his strategy.[33] He starts by rejecting Rousseau's idea of the social contract as the basis of the state. Instead, authority in any state really stems from the rational necessity for such a state, regardless of its supposed derivation, whether divine, contractual or patrimonial. The relations between government and the governed should be understood by the principle in Roman Law called 'negotiorum gestio'. Herzl the lawyer now explicates this theory, whereby any individual can act as a sort of guardian, a 'gestor', for another who is incapable for whatever reason of defending his or her own interests. There need be no actual human request or consent, 'higher necessity' is enough to justify the intervention of the self-appointed gestor on the behalf of the 'dominus'. 'Thus the gestor simply puts his hat on and goes forth.' The gestor takes on all liability for the dominus, and any approval is retrospective. This is how states actually function and obtain their legitimacy, argues Herzl, and this is how the state of the Jews will arise.

The Society of Jews will act as the gestor of the Jewish people, which, just like the dominus in legal theory, is politically rudderless and thus helpless. The Society is 'the new Moses of the Jews'; it will campaign to be recognized internationally as a 'state-creating power', and among Jews it will be 'the primal cell' of the state of the Jews.[34]

Having provided a convincing legal rationale for his movement, well suited to the élitist, politics-from-above attitude
already noted, Herzl then turns to the plans for settlement of
the land, which he envisages as being very orderly, and then
his ideas for the constitution of the new state. The choice is
between a democratic monarchy and an aristocratic republic,
of which he opts for the latter. The problem with the former
option is that Jewish history has been too discontinuous to
have a serious Jewish king nowadays. Without the balance of a
monarch, however, democracy has too many failings. This
conclusion should come as no surprise given Herzl's dim view
of French democratic politics. For Herzl democracy leads to a
loss of proportion in political judgement, to parliamentary
chatter, and to the horrible phenomenon of the career politician. Modern peoples are too complicated in their morals to
possess the 'political virtue' which Montesquieu saw as a
necessary requirement for a democratic system, and as Jews
are no different from other modern people, they are also not
suited to democracy. Besides, wrote Herzl, 'the first experience of freedom would at first make us far too arrogant.'
Referendums are also to be avoided, as 'the masses are even
worse than parliaments, for they allow themselves to be
influenced by every superstition, and fall for anyone who can
shout strongly.'

After this quite prescient critique of democracy, Herzl
suggests his idea of an 'aristocratic republic', which would
allow politics to be made from above, but would nevertheless
not enslave the populace, as it would be an open aristocracy,
with all given the chance to rise. In this way the ambitious
nature of the Jews, which is now reduced to foolish vanity,
would be given full rein to move up in society. Herzl thinks of
the Venetian model, but wants to avoid the faults which led to
that city-republic's demise. Jews should learn from the history
of others. The eventual constitution will be imposed on a
grateful people. As with some of his near contemporary
socialist thinkers, Herzl is clear that the opposition of 'narrow-
minded or malicious individuals' will not be tolerated.

There is then a short discussion of the language question, in which the option of Hebrew is decisively rejected—who, after all, can buy a railway ticket in Hebrew?—as well as Yiddish—'the furtive language of captives'. Instead the federal solution is again suggested, although this time German is not explicitly mentioned as the probable official language. This section leads on to a discussion of the place of religion in the new state, and here Herzl reveals his liberal and secular colours: 'Faith keeps us together; knowledge makes us free.' Religion and the army will thus be kept out of politics. Herzl goes on to say that the army will be a professional one, but the state will be neutral. The flag, very important in his view, will be white with seven gold stars, symbolizing the seven-hour day. In his last chapters he emphasizes two things: the Jews will fulfil all their outstanding debts to their host societies, whether financial or legal, and thus part honourably; also, the new land will, he reiterates, offer a model of social and technological progress, from which the rest of the world can learn. Europe, meanwhile, free of the burden of anti-Semitism, will prosper, and be an attractive home for Jewish capital.[35]

In the conclusion Herzl summarizes his argument, and counters more anticipated objections. That he is undermining the attempt to break down the barriers between peoples, to achieve a true fraternity, is an argument which Herzl not only claims is unrealistic—the fatherland will survive as an idea for centuries—it is not even a 'beautiful dream' as 'the enemy is necessary for the highest achievements of personality'. On the other hand he ends with the hope that what he is proposing will not only benefit the Jews, but will also be for the welfare of all Mankind.[36]

That these ideas—the survival of national difference as an inevitable and good thing, and the wish to contribute to the general progress of humanity—are not in contradiction, brings us to the central rationale that lies behind the 'practical' detail of Herzl's plan. What Herzl is saying in this pamphlet is what he has said in previous versions: that Jews are, as the anti-Semites rightly point out, different; that their life in Europe is thus based on false assumptions; and that it is thus an unhealthy influence, which must be remedied. Removal to their own land will not only remove the problem from Europe, it will also allow the Jews to liberate themselves from their past condition, and become not only a normal people, but a model one. As a people liberated from its past, the Jews can use the social and technological advances of the civilized world unencumbered by history. On the shoulders of the Western world, the Jews can show that world what lies beyond the horizon, and be in the vanguard of progress, respected and admired, one assumes, by the very world which once rejected them.

The first point should need little elaboration. Herzl, although prepared to allow a caveat for individuals, to help his political situation, clearly thought that the Jews were un-assimilable, and should not assimilate. Sometimes he seems to see this eternal Jewish identity as the result purely of what others think, a kind of negative identity: Jews are Jews because Gentiles see them as such. At other points, he sees a more positive identity; this is not a linguistic identity, nor is his Jewish identity explicitly racial.[37] Instead it appears to be one based on the principles of Jewish religion, hence his organizing the exodus around rabbis. Indeed at one point he has a three-tier Jewish identity: 'The personality of the Jewish people cannot, will not and must not disappear.'[38] It cannot disappear because the Gentiles will not let it (negative); it will not, because the Jews do not wish it (positive); and it must not (normative), because, it seems, it has a role to perform which Herzl wants to elaborate in the book. There is clearly something Herzl wants to preserve in Jewish identity, which can best be preserved in his state of the Jews.

If Jews remain different, then the ideology of emancipation, with its assumption that the Jews could be reformed to be acceptable and integrable citizens, is plainly mistaken. As such, Herzl is quite in agreement with anti-Semitic opponents of emancipation, and blames anti-Semitism squarely on the unrealistic hopes of the emancipationists. Yet his recognition of this failure leads him to discuss the need for a new state, as a direct response to anti-Semitism. The state of the Jews is at once a proof of Jewish identity and the true consequence of emancipation, the way to real inner freedom.

It is, I think, no accident that Herzl is tempted to discuss the 'human resources' at his disposal at this point in his argument, for his goal is not only to respond to anti-Semitism, it is also to provide the final remedy to the Jewish condition which the age of oppression had created and the age of emancipation had failed to ameliorate. When he does discuss Jewish 'human resources', he shows a much increased confidence in the character of Jews, the result of his greater experience of Jews since beginning his Zionist campaign in July, no doubt, and the need to sell his plan to the Jewish masses. Now Jews are misunderstood rather than truly degenerate. They are not even particularly commercially-minded, let alone a 'people of stockbrokers'.[39] Yet Herzl still wants to ensure that they are encouraged not to have to indulge in petty trading. Hence his wish to have great department stores provide for the state's commercial needs. The idea that this new state will bring about a moral regeneration of the Jews is somewhat muted compared to earlier versions, but it is still there. The ideology of the emancipation has been transferred abroad.

At one point Herzl remarks on the fact that, apart from the rich, most Jews have few links with Christians. 'In many lands the situation is such that the Jew who does not maintain a couple of spongers, borrowers and "Jew-slaves" knows absolutely no Christians. The ghetto continues to exist inwardly.'[40] Ostensibly this is a reference to the lack of social integration, which will make leaving Europe less wrenching. Yet it is also a reminder of Herzl's former, moral interpretation of the 'new ghetto'. The state of the Jews, in contrast, is a state where Jews are not only allowed to be Jews, they are also to be allowed to be model citizens of a model state. Not only will the exodus take place 'in the midst of civilization', and the customs and habits of the former Western homes (including the Viennese coffeehouse) brought over for people to feel at home; more than that, things will be 'better, more beautiful and more comfortable'. And if the environment will thus be an improved version of the West, so will the populace. There will be no beggary, for all will be assured work in the new system of labour assistance, made possible by the *tabula rasa* nature of the new society. Beggary indeed will not be tolerated. There will be a proto-welfare state to take care of the sick and the 'deserving poor'. The work-shy will end up in workhouses. Some allowance must, admittedly, be made for the weaknesses of the present generation, 'but the future generations should be raised differently, in freedom for freedom.'[41] The aim will be to provide everyone with the 'moral bliss of work'. 'In this way our people will rediscover its industriousness in the land of the seven-hour day.' The worthy citizens of a liberal (if not democratic, and rather patriarchal) state will thus deserve to be part of Western civilization. The integration of the Jews into the modern world will be effected, not by them as individuals but as a nation.

Indeed the state of the Jews will be a paragon of modernity. As Herzl says of his plans for the constitution, 'For we are a modern people, and want to be the most modern.'[42] This is evident in his 'progressive' social ideas, but also in his emphasis on technology. Even his cultural metaphors reveal a technological bent. When comparing the Society, the new gestor, to the old, Moses, Herzl likens this to the difference between an old *Singspiel* and a modern opera: 'We play the same melody, but with many, many more violins, flutes, harps, cellos and basses, electric light, decorations, choirs, wonderful production and the best singers.'[43] Indeed his introduction starts with a paean to the possibilities opened up by the advance of technology. One of the major possibilities of the new age is that Jews, who are not known as manual workers, will not need to become so, because the machines will be their 'work-slaves'. Electric light was invented, says Herzl, so that the problems of Mankind could be solved by its light, among them the Jewish question. He returns to the merits of technology just before his conclusion. Electricity is discussed here again, this time as the solution to the 'social question', the remedy to 'steam' which created so much social pressure. He enthuses about the speed with which cities are built in America, and the way 'we moderns' are able to 'turn the desert into a garden'.[44] If Herzl wants to turn his state into a 'model state' of social progress, he also wants it to be a model of technological advance. A comment in his diary perhaps sums up Herzl's devotion to the modern, technological world: reminded of the failure of Shabbetai Zvi's attempt to regain the Promised Land, he said: 'Yes, in a former century it was impossible. Now it is possible. Because we have machines.'[45]

The state of the Jews not only owes a debt to Western social thought and technology; the whole concept is deeply indebted to Western thought, as Herzl is quite aware. There is the use of Roman law, already noted above. Then again, Herzl's liberal interpretation of nationalism puts him in a very prominent Western tradition, of Herder, Mazzini, and others, such as the Austrian (and Jewish) political thinker Adolf Fischhof.[46]

More fundamentally than this, however, the very need for a state, in the view of Joseph Adler, stems from Herzl's understanding of Hegelian thought, as mediated by his university professor, Lorenz von Stein.[47] It was also Stein who was partly responsible for the idea of a 'legal' and a 'moral' person, which was to determine the shape of the future Zionist movement, and seems to have derived from Herzl's studies of Austrian law under Stein. The other major influence on Herzl's legal underpinning of his state idea was, huge irony, the codifier of Austrian law, Joseph Unger, an Austrian minister of justice and converted Jew.[48]

Beyond this influence of his legal training, the great emphasis on legality which characterizes Der Judenstaat, and subsequently the whole of Herzl's Zionist strategy, depends for much of its force on another Western view of the state, a principle older than Hegelian state theory: namely the principle of the Rechtsstaat, the state of law. This had been a central concept of the German Enlightenment, and a major part of the Jewish ideology of emancipation. Indeed, in its guarantee of equal rights under the law, it was fundamental to that ideology. Herzl's state of the Jews, as the final realization of proper emancipation, is in some ways no more than the final achievement of a true state of law, where there is no *de facto* discrimination, that is to say breach of the law's impartiality.

It should be added here for future reference that when he proposed an international solution to what had been seen as an intra-national problem, Herzl also brought the idea of the state of law, an integral part of the ideology of emancipation, to this higher, international level. His state of the Jews had thus to be founded within a legal, albeit now international, framework. In so doing Herzl revealed himself to be much more a Kantian than a Hegelian in his attitude to the rule of law on the international stage. Herzl's subsequent insistence in his Zionist campaign on the legal recognition of the Jewish homeland by the international community as a *sine qua non* of settlement, a viewpoint which marks his particular brand of 'political Zionism' out from others, was in this way a powerful legacy of the Central European Jewish ideology of emancipation, and the thought of the German Enlightenment which had so inspired that ideology.[49]

The discussion of the concept of the *Rechtsstaat* brings us to the centre of Herzl's new, Zionist vision: the principle of tolerance. With deep dialectical irony, Herzl explicitly identifies this principle as one learnt from the West. The Jews were given emancipation; now, in their own state they must live up to this great gift. Thus, when discussing the need to keep religion out of politics, he takes the position that everyone be allowed to be as free in their religion as in their nationality (by which he means language). 'And if it so happens that persons of another faith, of another nation, live among us, we shall guarantee them honourable protection and equality before the law. We learnt tolerance in Europe.'[50]

What is so deeply ironic about this viewpoint is that Herzl sees this realization of the Western principle of tolerance as the new mission of the Jews, for which they have been singled out by fate, even by a kind of providence. (One should perhaps recall here the reaction in his diary to the idea that the Jews could form a 'model state': 'What a gift of God to the Jews!') By instituting the rule of tolerance in their own state the Jews will finally realize for themselves the aim of inner freedom, as well as the promise of 'honour, freedom and happiness'. Yet the achievement by the Jews of a truly tolerant, emancipated society, combined with the prosperity provided by its economic, social and technological sophistication, will serve not only the Jews themselves, but the whole world. 'The world will be freed through our freedom, enriched by our wealth, and made greater by our greatness. And what we do there only for our own prosperity, will have a powerful and beneficial effect on the welfare of all Mankind.'[51]

Herzl has indeed found a new purpose for the 'personality of the Jewish people', and it is not only the self-emancipation of the Jews, but the emancipation of Mankind itself. Herzl thus manages to invent a prospective Jewish identity whose particularity is its emancipatory universalism. While realizing their identity as Jews, and reuniting their nation in their own state, the Jews are not going to reject all that they learnt in the West; they are going to improve on it. They are going to become, as Herzl put it, the 'most modern' people in the world, the most free and the most advanced, a veritable 'light unto the nations'. The only difference from the emancipatory version of the 'Jewish mission' is that now the Jews will be a nation among other nations, rather than a group of people dispersed around the globe. That in saying this he was more or less echoing, unwittingly, the thought of Moses Hess, only indicates how much he was indebted, as Hess before him, to the emancipatory tradition of Central European Jewry.[52]

4

POLITICAL LIFE

In the midst of his surge of inspiration in early June 1895, Herzl wrote that gambling would be forbidden in the new state, because the spirit of adventure should not be so wasted, but instead channelled into developing the new land. He admitted that 'I myself was a gambler in my youth,' but added: 'I only gambled because I had no way to satisfy my urge to action.'[1] Now, with Zionism, Herzl had found an excellent way to do this. The Jewish journalist in him, and he saw the Jewish journalist as the only kind of Jew who knew anything about politics, now had the chance after which he had hankered for some time. What had been denied him as an Austrian was now possible by being a Jew, the leader of a Jewish movement: Herzl became a politician.

By the time *Der Judenstaat* was published, Herzl was already well into his 'campaign', as he proudly called it. From the start he had adopted the persona of a 'politician', at one stage even 'a statesman, and a Jewish one at that'. Furthermore, he had had early premonitions of his place in history: 'Today a single and lonely man, tomorrow perhaps the spiritual leader of hundreds of thousands. In any case the discoverer and proclaimer of a mighty idea.' His lasting fame, which he had always craved, had been assured, for 'life has stopped and world history has begun.'[2] After having tried and failed to win the backing of Hirsch, Bismarck, or Albert Rothschild, he had attempted to gain the confidential support of various prominent Jews, including the Chief Rabbi of Vienna, Moritz Güdemann, various bankers, and, most importantly in Herzl's view at this stage, his editors-in-chief at the *Neue Freie Presse*,

Eduard Bacher and Moritz Benedikt. It is typical of Herzl that his main strategy for his political campaign was to have a deal between the powers and the Jewish establishment struck behind closed doors, and then the *fait accompli* announced in the *Neue Freie Presse*.[3] The significance he placed in his newspaper can be measured by the fact that to Herzl his discussion in October with Benedikt on the walk to Mauer was a—yet another—historic turning point. Everything before had been 'dreams and mere words', now: 'The deed has begun, because I shall either have the *Neue Freie Presse* with me, or against me.' His editors proved eventually to be against him, despite an apparent ambivalence on the Jewish question.[4] By now, however, Herzl was completely committed to his 'idea', and, after travelling to Paris and England, where he gained further supporters, including Max Nordau, Colonel Goldsmid and Israel Zangwill, Herzl finally put the cat among the pigeons and published *Der Judenstaat*. Even the repeated admonition of Benedikt, that no individual could take it upon himself to 'start this avalanche, which endangers so many interests', could not stop Herzl from making his 'idea' 'day and deed'.[5]

From the publication of *Der Judenstaat* on, Herzl's life reads more like a fantasy spy novel than a real life. It is a biographer's dream to write the life of someone who saw so many of his personal dreams fulfilled in the way Herzl did. His 'campaign' on behalf of Zionism was, by any measure, a phenomenal performance, which brought him into the courts and inner circles of most of the governments of Europe, and put political Zionism on the map of international politics. Not only that, he managed to give the Jewish people, if not a state, at least a congress and a 'Jewish Colonial Trust', the 'moral' and 'legal' forms which he had adumbrated in *Der Judenstaat*.

Between the spring of 1896 and the summer of 1902 Herzl toured the courts of Europe in pursuit of his goals. Fairly early on he seems to have realized that the goal had to be Palestine. The strategy he adopted was to seek a deal with the Ottoman sultan, whereby 'the Jews' would solve the Turks' fiscal crisis in return for the granting of land for the Jews' state, or, as it became, 'homeland'. As a guarantee, and a way of putting pressure on the Turks, he would persuade the powers of Europe, most importantly Germany (from the Hirsch notes on at the centre of his diplomatic strategy) followed by England, to support his plan, and give it official recognition. This would result in international safeguards for the future state's security. At all times Herzl was convinced that the only way of achieving a viable state of the Jews in Palestine was by 'political' means, that is to say by obtaining official, public recognition from the international community for the Jews' state, by being above board. In contrast, the policy of 'infiltration', of gradual colonization without any official sanction, or 'crawling in' as Herzl was wont to describe it, would only cause more problems. It would certainly not produce the universal reconciliation between the Jews and their enemies which was all along his aim.[6] His diplomatic campaigning was thus much more than a way of satisfying his urge to consort with 'the high-ups'. It had a very serious, indeed perceptive, purpose behind it.

His entrée into the society of European princes was found through the unlikely figure of William Hechler, an Anglican clergyman, who introduced Herzl to Friedrich, Grand Duke of Baden, the first of Herzl's diplomatic contacts and one of his most steadfast, if secret, patrons. Another important figure in Herzl's diplomatic campaign was the rather shady Polish nobleman, Philip de Nevlinski, who provided contacts with the Ottoman court in Constantinople, to which Herzl went on the first of several visits in the summer of 1896. The high point of Herzl's diplomacy came with his audience with Kaiser Wilhelm II in Constantinople in the autumn of 1898. Admittedly the Sultan vehemently opposed the idea and so made it impossible, but it is a remarkable fact that Wilhelm was apparently prepared to make the Jewish state a German protectorate. Herzl, who was a great admirer of the German emperor, revealed how little his admiration for German culture had been lessened since his student days: 'Being under the protectorate of this strong, great, moral, superbly administered and rigorously organized Germany, can only have the most salutary effect on the Jewish national character.'[7] Despite an impromptu encounter with the emperor in Palestine (at a Rothschild colony), and a symbolic address to him outside the walls of Jerusalem, nothing came of this plan—one of modern history's larger 'what-ifs'.

Herzl did not give up. In 1901 he was again in Constantinople, this time being received by the Sultan Abdul Hamid II himself. The following year saw renewed negotiations with the Turks over a 'charter', without success. In a deep depression over this failure, he saw himself as 'the Yid who was summoned' so that the Turks could bargain for a better deal.[8] This was true, but it should not mask the fact that merely to be in that situation was a great achievement: Herzl had made Zionism, almost single-handedly, a player in international diplomacy.

If his efforts at diplomacy were impressive, but, due to the implacable opposition of the Turks, ultimately without concrete results, Herzl's campaign within the Jewish world did produce results of historic import. Chief among these was the meeting of the First Zionist Congress in Basel in August 1897. How Herzl managed to bring about this unheard-of event, which was to be the basis of a national assembly of the Jews, had a great deal to do with his characteristically iron insistence that the congress be held, whoever turned up, and with the deft handling by him and his now faithful lieutenant Max Nordau of the storm of controversy which followed the original announcement of the meeting in March 1897. Typical of Herzl was his founding of a Zionist weekly journal, *Die Welt*, in June 1897, largely in order to publicize the congress. Typical as well was his original hesitancy in appealing to the Russian 'lovers of Zion', until the refusal of Western Jewish 'notables' to attend required a larger Russian presence to make good the shortfall. That he did call on the Russians, and that they came, albeit with conditions, was a major turning point in the history of Zionism.

After the mighty struggle to make sure it happened at all,

the congress itself was an astounding success, providing a forum for world Jewry which proved that the Jews were indeed a nation. As Herzl himself put it, with a certain amount of insight: 'in Basel I founded the state of the Jews.'[9] As we shall see, he was greatly helped in this task by the fact that Zionism had already been in existence for some years when he 'discovered' it. Nevertheless, in having the willpower and the sheer *chutzpah* to set up the congress, and to organize the subsequent meetings until the fateful sixth congress of 1903, Herzl achieved an organizational miracle which might not have come about without him. Further, his insistence that the Jews set up his Jewish Company led to the foundation in 1899 of the Jewish Colonial Trust, which was to become the Zionist bank and the parent of Bank Leumi. As in so many of Herzl's achievements, the fact that this bank was never a financial success in his lifetime is insignificant beside the fact that he managed to create the practical framework of a national movement which, by his death, was being taken seriously on the international stage. Through Herzl, Zionism gained a united leadership, a voice, and revenue, or at least the makings of these.

Herzl on occasion considered what it was that he contributed to the Zionist movement. At one point he thought it was 'prestige', at another the fact of his selflessness. At other moments it seemed to him that his effort alone was keeping the cause going.[10] His greatest contribution, however, was probably that, for all his eccentricities and fantasies, he had a strong grip on the realities of modern politics. His efforts to set up a congress, a Zionist press and a bank came from the insight that these were absolute necessities for a national movement, if it was to gain respect and recognition. That all three were somewhat fragile was something which Herzl would have seen as regrettable but irrelevant, for their existence was what mattered. These were the 'imponderables' which Herzl thought of as the crucial element of politics. His description of how he founded the Jewish state at Basel illustrates this view: 'The state is essentially based on the wish of the people, or even a powerful enough individual, . . . for a state. Territory is only the concrete foundation; the state itself, even where it has territory, is always something abstract.' 'In Basel I have thus created,' he claimed, 'this abstract part, which is invisible to most people. Actually I did it with infinitesimally small means. I gradually incited the people into the state mood, and made them feel that they were at a national assembly.'[11] In this description of the political process, what is important is not substance but abstract ideas, not argument but the manipulation of feelings—this is the modern political world where 'imponderable' aspects such as ideas, moods and feelings are all.

There is little doubt that Herzl had developed over the years a fairly acute sense of what modern politics—the 'politics of the new key'—were about.[12] That he saw the 'old' politics of rational and moderate debate on substantive topics as outmoded is clear as early as 1893, with his advice to Leitenberger to avoid letting any new journal be as 'boring' as the German Liberal press, and his insistence on the necessity of a 'movement'. We have already seen him advocating the power of 'imponderables' in his notes for Hirsch. As so often, Herzl seems to have had the German example foremost in his mind here, as shown by his subsequent admonition to Hirsch about the importance of a flag: 'With a flag one can lead human beings where one will, even into the Promised Land. For a flag they will live and die; indeed it is the only thing for which the masses are prepared to die—if one educates them to that.' 'Believe me,' he continued, 'the politics of a whole people—especially when it is so dispersed throughout the whole world—can only be conducted through imponderables, which float in the air. Do you know how the German empire was created? From day-dreams, songs, fantasies and black-red-gold ribands. And in short order. Bismarck only shook the tree, which the dreamers had planted.'[13] He was equally perceptive when he advised Koerber that an invented enemy was almost as effective as a real one in electoral politics.[14] His plans to use high culture, festivals and pro-

cessions to build national consciousness, and his conviction
that one could only communicate with the crowd in simple
symbols, also reveal a real insight into the motivation of the
masses.[15] He was always an artist-politician.

Herzl's was also undoubtedly a politics of the will. He had a
firm faith that the human will could accomplish virtually
anything, and that dreams could be realized, if only people
could be properly motivated.[16] Above all, and here he
reflected the Schillerian tradition in German liberalism more
than anything else, he believed in the power of ideas, or rather
his idea—of the state of the Jews. The faith which he often fell
back on in the 'inevitability' of that idea often smacks of
wishful thinking rather than true conviction, as though it was
inevitable because it *had* to be inevitable.[17] On the other hand,
the very act of willing oneself to believe in something which
at first sight was unrealizable was a facet of the kind of
charismatic leader into which Herzl turned himself. His confidence that he could 'grow' with the movement (another
Schillerian idea)[18] was symptomatic of Herzl's belief that he
had become a man of destiny. Perhaps this also explains why,
from the start, he had complete confidence that he could
'conquer the people', 'lead them where I will'.[19] The irony
was that he was right, and part of the reason he was able to
carry the crowd with him was not so much his rather forced
ideas about the 'theory of the crowd', but rather that he had
the confidence that he could indeed lead them. Herzl's
renowned ability to enthuse the masses was to a certain extent
a self-fulfilling prophecy.

Perhaps the most often repeated quotation in Herzl's diaries
is from Virgil's *Aeneid*: 'Flectere si nequeo superos, Acheronta
movebo.' ('If I cannot bend the higher powers, I shall stir up
hell.')[20] If Freud's famous use of this quotation was ambivalent, Herzl's was as straightforward as that by Lassalle, one of
his role models. Lassalle had meant to threaten the Prussian
regime with the spectre of national revolution if it did not lead
the national cause.[21] Herzl, similarly, used the Jewish masses as
a threat against the Jewish establishment, whether it be the

Rothschilds or the *Neue Freie Presse*. He did this with the confidence gained from his various experiences of mass adulation, and his often proven ability to bring a crowd to great, almost hysterical, enthusiasm. His prestige, his dramatic and commanding presence, and his ponderous but impressive delivery made him into a speaker of considerable mass appeal. That someone had shouted out in the synagogue in Sofia that he was 'more important than the Torah' must have given Herzl an immense confidence that he could control the crowd.[22] Certainly this is where he was to find most of his support, among the Jewish masses, and the élitist Herzl of the early period did give way to a leader more sensitive to the 'little man' in European Jewry and more prepared to 'stir up hell' by appealing to the mass of Jews, as his 'shekel' campaign and his strategy of 'conquering the communities' by a populist politics show. To that extent he clearly became a politician of the 'new key'.

Yet Herzl was an extremely reluctant populist, let alone demagogue.[23] Quoting Virgil was one thing, actually implementing the threat was quite another, and Herzl never really did. He was far too concerned with preserving law and order, far too much the liberal intellectual, too much his father's son, to want to be a true exponent of mass, irrationalist politics. There was an immense gap between what he thought in private, and what he allowed the public to hear. The diary was written without 'self-criticism', but his public statements, especially *Der Judenstaat*, are written with a very self-critical pen, and the exclusion of all the more fanciful ideas. He explicitly exercised a great deal of self-control.[24] In his diplomacy, perhaps not surprisingly, he would say what pleased his audience: to the Austrians that Germany was the real centre of anti-Semitism, to the Grand Duke of Baden that Austria was the problem. He was also quite prepared to leave people, such as a certain Hasid who thought he was a Wunderrabbi, with their illusions. Similarly, he was careful to keep the full truth of his intentions from the public, which he felt should be led unwittingly to its redemption.[25] When he threatened to 'stir up hell' he did so really only as a threat, to get the 'great in Israel' to go along with him. That he repeated the threat at least four times shows both how impervious the establishment was, and also how reluctant Herzl was to give up hope in the Jewish élite.[26]

Herzl was forced into entering the realm of mass politics, but he professed a certain cynicism about it. He was an irrationalist politician in his head, but not in his heart. He understood how to produce enthusiasm in a crowd, yet it left him cold. He knew the importance of 'noise' in politics, yet what was important was 'to use it—and nevertheless despise it'. Despite the fact that he fervently believed in the power of the human will, he thought Nietzsche's ideas to be the thoughts of a madman.[27]

Herzl was insistent that his Zionist movement must be seen as not only practical, but also legal and civilized. His whole strategy, very much that of a qualified doctor of law and deeply influenced by the emphasis put on the *Rechtsstaat* and the rule of law in the Central European ideology of emancipation, depended on gaining international legal recognition for his state of the Jews, or, as the Basel Congress famously termed it, 'a home for the Jewish people in Palestine secured by public law'. It was imperative that the world be convinced that the Zionists 'neither foster haughty dreams, nor want anything foolish or unjust', for Herzl thought that only an honest, upright people could demand international respect.[28] It certainly made public relations sense when Herzl insisted in his speeches, interviews and articles that Zionism represented the Jewish people's 'will to law and order', that it was no retreat from progress, but was rather 'a moral, legal and philanthropic movement', full of 'the desire for legality'.[29] Yet this was more than just Herzl's public image; when he stated that the movement could not be based on dreams of military conquest, but had to be based instead on 'the ground of reason' and 'practical politics', he was also reflecting his private thoughts, for his diaries show the same emphasis on the need for order, rationality, moderation, and progress.[30]

It is actually very difficult on occasion to separate the politician of the new key from the liberal believer in progress. One example cited as evidence of Herzl's belief in the dynamic, new key politics of 'movement' is his metaphor of the secret of flight: 'Great things need no firm foundation. An apple must be placed on the table to keep it from falling. The earth hovers in the air. Thus I can perhaps found and secure the state of the Jews without any firm anchorage. The secret lies in movement. Hence I believe that somewhere a guidable aircraft will be discovered. Gravity overcome through movement.'[31] Schorske has emphasized the idea of Herzl founding a 'movement' here, but it is just as easy to stress the technological aspect of Herzl's obsession with the possibility of manned flight. That he used 'The guidable aircraft' as the metaphor for Zionism in an article of the same name shows Herzl's identification of his movement as ultra-modern and progressive, a great boon to Mankind.[32] (He often saw Zionism as a modern machine fuelled by Jewish need and Jewish desires.) That the metaphor continues, 'and not the ship, but the ship's movement is to be guided' also shows Herzl's wish to guide, and thus control, his mass movement. This is as much a technically minded, progressive liberal speaking as a politician of the new key.

Even Herzl's theatricality, the essence of his 'artist-political' nature, was used in the interests of 'culture', by which he meant civilization. Güdemann once likened Herzl to an 'operetta general' and, as we have seen, he was prone to fanciful and dramatic images. He himself was well aware of this side to his character: 'And actually I am still as ever the dramatist in all this. I take poor, destitute people off the street, dress them in wonderful clothes, and have them perform before the world a marvellous play of mine.'[33] Herzl always emphasized the significance of dress, and of 'externalities'; what one wore was of crucial significance to a former dandy (and snob) such as Herzl. Yet it is very interesting to see what kind of clothes he dressed his people in, and for what reason.

We have seen him attempt an emancipatory symbolism

with his 'Doge' coronation ceremony, and create an aristocracy with his yellow riband. Two further examples show
Herzl attempting, through dress, to maintain the civilized
order of his liberal, bourgeois modernity. The first occurs
when he is envisaging life aboard the ship sent to claim the
new Jewish land. He wants all passengers on board to wear
black tie at dinner, in order, he explains, that people do not see
themselves as going into a desert, but instead recognize that
'culture' is going with them.[34] Black tie is here a symbol of
civilization, as it indeed was in the imperial colonies of the age.
This was a prescription which Herzl never implemented, but
the second example was put into effect in a legendary manner.
When Herzl called the Zionist congress in Basel in 1897, he
insisted that all delegates wear white tie. He forced even a
reluctant Nordau to wear the dress of festivities (and diplomatic congresses). He did so, he wrote in his diary, because he
wanted the people to feel 'stiff'; thus would arise a 'measured
tone' which he could then raise to a level of solemnity.[35] In
other words, Herzl's dress sense was being employed in the
interests of sobriety, moderation and solemnity, to control the
crowd.

What makes Herzl remarkable is that, while he recognized
the power of 'imponderables' and 'externalities' in the same
way as other modern, charismatic politicians, he saw how
they could be used to preserve exactly the kind of liberal social
order which his counterparts threatened. If dress could be used
to preserve the liberal order, so could other external forms.
When he went to visit the English poet laureate, Alfred
Austin, in 1900 Herzl remarked on the impressive formalities
of English life. 'The foolish revolutionaries despise old forms
and externalities. But the spruce table, the well-kept house,
and the well-mannered coachman also have their significance.
The form which has arisen from the content through the
never-ending labour of many generations, has in turn shaped
that content.'[36] In other words, England's liberal order sus-
tained itself, in Herzl's view, by the very formalities it had
created for itself. Content could thus be determined by form,

whether it be dress, manners, public image or an organizational structure. What was important was to make the form suitable for the desired content, which in Herzl's view should be a liberal, modern and progressive one.

Herzl said of himself once, 'I am simply a modern and thus natural person, without affectations. I am conducting my campaign without follies, without any fanatical posturings.'[37] As will already have become evident, this was a little disingenuous. Yet in another, more fundamental way, he was only telling the truth; his aim was always to make his insights into the power of image, form and appearance in modern mass politics serve the purpose of making Zionism, his movement, into a respectable and permanent institution. It was indeed not with 'fanatical' but rather with reasonable, moderate and practical 'posturings' that he intended to lead his movement to the Promised Land. The irony of Herzl's rationale for setting up the congress and the bank was that they were both part of his tactic of making outward forms influence and create content, and they were also a way of providing an 'impersonal' structure to guarantee that the movement would survive his leadership.[38] Even though these institutions might lack substance, what was important was that people perceived they existed and could organize themselves around them, knowing, or at least sensing, that here were permanent institutions with a future. Herzl was thus using the politics of dynamism to create permanence. But more than this, these institutions were also part of his attempt to give his movement legitimacy and the appearance of solidity, to make it look like the harbinger of a respectable, liberal and constitutional state. With the insights of a modern artist-politician, Herzl thus designed a movement which was not only liberal in its goals, but also liberal in its form, and hence, he hoped, its content.

If Herzl preserved liberalism by exploiting the methods of the new post-liberal politics, he also attempted to maintain his liberal, emancipatory interpretation of Jewishness in the face of his new experience of Jews, and what being Jewish meant. If his life was transformed after June 1895 by his entry into the world of politics, it was also radically changed by his exposure to the world of European, especially Eastern European, Jewry. As he said himself, when he started his Zionist campaign, 'I was still a stranger to my people.'[39] He knew little about the Jewish religion, or at least had forgotten most of what he knew. Moreover, he was unaware of the plight of 'our poor masses', and claimed to know nothing of the 'recent movements' in Jewish life, that is to say Zionism (although diary entries suggest he had an inkling of their existence). Over the following years he did much to remedy this situation, but always in his own way, on his own terms.

Herzl's idea of religion at the start of his Zionist years owed something to Judaism, but, as with many similar children of the emancipation and assimilation, his was an extremely abstract notion of divinity. The word 'God', for him, was 'this dear, old, wonderful abbreviation, through which I come to terms with the oneness of the world.' When expounding his theories to Rabbi Güdemann he equated God with the 'will to good'; for him the 'historical' God was merely a way to explain a complex idea to children. Herzl himself claimed to have a Spinozan understanding of God, but with a concept of the will added. 'The world is the body,' he opined, 'and God is the function.'[40] With such an abstract, almost secular understanding of religion, it is not all that surprising that he was unabashed when Güdemann visited the Herzl household on Christmas Eve 1895 and found him lighting the candles on the 'Christmas tree'. 'As far as I am concerned,' responded Herzl, 'it can be called the Hanukkah tree—or the winter solstice?'[41]

Herzl never became religious in the proper sense of the word. He did, however, come greatly to appreciate Jewish traditions, and on several occasions was clearly deeply moved by participation in Jewish religious ceremonies, an instance being his appearance at the synagogue in Basel in 1897.[42] A particularly revealing article on Herzl's relationship to Jewish religious tradition is the transparently autobiographical piece 'The Menorah' of December 1897. Here the protagonist, an artist who has returned to Judaism, realizes that he is too assimilated into Western society to become fully Jewish. Yet he hopes to bring his children up so that they at least can be real Jews. (Herzl taught his children to recite Hebrew prayers.) For his children's sake he has a Hanukkah menorah (candelabrum) in the house, which he comes to love for what it tells him 'above his understanding'. In other words, he realizes what he had never expected, the beauty of the Jewish tradition. As an artist he feels compelled to draw a modern version of the menorah, and then, with all its nine candles burning, he recognizes it as a symbol of 'the bursting into flame of the nation'. The lighting of one candle at a time is symbolic of the way the Zionist idea has spread, starting with the young and the poor and spreading to the whole nation. 'No office is more felicitous,' adds Herzl in conclusion, 'than being the servant of light.'[43] By thus seeing himself as the ninth candle of the menorah, with which all the other candles are lighted, Herzl is not only showing the great change from his attitude to Hanukkah a mere two years before, but also identifying religious tradition with himself, and with his cause.

This identification cut both ways. His identification of religion as symbolic of the nation was balanced by his quasi-religious belief in the significance of his own mission. He is never very insistent on the point, but there are moments in his diaries when his language suggests that he saw himself as divinely inspired. The characterization of the state of the Jews as 'a gift of God' is one such occasion. That he speaks in 1899 of returning to the hotel in Paris where he had received his inspiration 'out of piety' is another.[44] Beneath Herzl's 'secular nationalism' was a strong undercurrent of divine mission, albeit in Herzl's abstract understanding of the term. Religious in the strict sense he may not have been, but that he felt himself on a divinely inspired mission of redemption is more than likely.[45]

Herzl's return to Judaism was also a return to the Jewish people. He would occasionally see Zionism as a two-stage process, with 'a coming home to Judaism before the return to the Jewish land'. He spoke once to the student group Kadimah of the 'inner Zion' which could be realized now, while the real Zion was awaited.[46] Herzl himself showed his new Jewish identity by a greater use of Yiddish expressions, albeit usually in jest. His confidence that he could now discern the different Jewish 'types' also suggests his belief, or his wish to believe, that he belonged once more.[47] This does not mean that his dislike of the world of the assimilated Viennese Jewish bourgeoisie declined. Instead the people who had once typified 'the Jew' for him were seen as the false Jews. As he put it in his diary, there were 'Jiden' and 'Juden', Yids and Jews, and his cause was for the latter, not the former.[48]

Part of this reaction was a result of his disappointment at his rejection by the Jewish establishment. It should be noted here that this rejection was quite understandable. While the prevalence of anti-Semitism throughout most of the Continent, and especially in Herzl's home town of Vienna, was a severe setback to hopes of a successful and trouble-free integration into Gentile society, the situation did not appear to most people as hopeless as it did to Herzl. In Germany and France (after the victory of the pro-Dreyfus forces in 1899) it even seemed that the storm had passed. In any case, most in the Jewish financial and cultural élite were relatively untouched by anti-Semitic riots or boycotts, and, furthermore, too firmly and genuinely committed to their respective national identities to think of supporting Zionism.

In contrast, Herzl's appeared a madcap scheme with little chance of success, ripe for the kind of biting satire which Karl Kraus expended in his *Eine Krone für Zion* (A Crown for Zion), or the more balanced critique which Arthur Schnitzler, Herzl's former confidant, was to include in his novel *Der Weg ins Freie* (The Road to the Open).[49] Seen from an assimilatory perspective, Zionism was not only futile but positively dangerous, for in positing a Jewish *national* identity Zionism, especially Herzl's Zionism, also effectively denied the acquired national identities of Jewish Frenchmen, Englishmen,

Germans, Austrians and the rest. What was worse was that the
Zionist claim tended to rebound against all Jews, thus threatening the degree of integration and acceptance they had
already achieved. Unless they accepted Herzl's theories completely, it made no sense to support him even partially. Herzl
must have realized how much he was demanding, and cannot
have been too surprised at the resistance he encountered.
Nevertheless he was clearly embittered by the rejection of his
visionary solution.

This was, however, not the only reason for Herzl's often
repeated attack on 'bad' Jews. The fact is that it also neatly
fitted into his previous view of the Jewish question, and his
present one. The epitome of this 'Zionist anti-Semitism' was
his diatribe 'Mauschel', in which he divided Jews into real
Jews and a 'lower' Mauschel race. Mauschel is simply Herzl's
former negative view of Jews: dishonest, vain, trying to
disappear into society, with no sense of honour and only
interested in making money. The real Jews are those with a
proud sense of Jewish identity and honour, such as Herzl has
discovered.[50] Herzl regretted publishing this piece in a fit of
pique, but it still says much about the way his new Jewish
identity served his past hates and his need for self-respect.

The contrast to the Mauschels of this world was provided
by the Zionist movement. Herzl came to his Zionist idea as a
solution to the Jewish problem as he understood it: the failure
of the assimilation of Jews in Western and Central Europe. He
initially thought he had invented Zionism, as a political
movement if not the ancient idea itself; he had, after all, not
even read George Eliot's *Daniel Deronda*. He soon came to
realize, when informed of the works of Moses Hess, Nathan
Birnbaum and Leon Pinsker ('Pinsger' in Herzl's diary entry),
and of the group Hovevei Zion, the Lovers of Zion, that
Zionism, as idea and movement, had pre-dated his 'conversion' by some years.[51] If, through Zionism, Herzl solved his
own personal conflicts by externalizing the dialectic of his
'inner' ghetto, the revelation of the already existing movement, and its specific, very different character, left him strug-

gling for the rest of his life with a new confrontation. This was between his own liberal, secular and emancipatory ideas, shared by his Western and Central European supporters, and those of the pre-existing Zionists, largely based in Russia, which were much more influenced by religious ideas, even if in secular garb, and which contained a much stronger sense of Jewish cultural identity.

The already established Zionists, deeply influenced by the Russian form of the *Haskalah* (Jewish Enlightenment) rather than the German form which was at the base of Herzl's ideological background, put much more emphasis on the substantial content of what it meant to be Jewish. Above all, in the 'cultural Zionism' of Ahad Ha'am, the restitution of Hebrew as a living language was a major goal, one quite alien to Herzl. Similarly, whereas Herzl started out thinking that a new land, such as Argentina, was acceptable, even a Westerner like Colonel Goldsmid immediately pointed out to him that only Palestine could be the goal.[52] That this pre-existing Zionism had also been the motive force for the 'infiltration' which, as we have seen, Herzl thought was ill-advised, if not actually harmful to the cause, was also going to be a major source of contention. On the other hand, it was the Eastern European Jews, whether they were in the shtetls of Russia and Galicia, in the East End of London, or in Jewish fraternities in Western universities, such as Kadimah in Vienna, who pro-vided Herzl with most of his support, and gave him the 'Jewish masses' with which he could threaten the Jewish establishment. Whether he liked it or not, therefore, Herzl had to come to terms with this revelation, the world of East European Jewry.

In some ways Herzl was clearly very impressed by the leaders of Russian Zionism. In an interview given after the Basel congress, Herzl praised the participants from the east. Instead of being 'a kind of Caliban' and culturally inferior, these Russian Jews had turned out to be as well educated as their Western counterparts, while retaining the 'inner unity' which Western Jews had lost. These modern ghetto Jews thus had the best of both worlds, being 'upright and authentic'.[53] Part of this positive attitude was clearly Herzl's attempt at good public relations with his new allies, even given the somewhat patronizing approach. On the other hand, much of it was heartfelt, for this kind of Jew, modern and yet still Jewish, was exactly the kind of Jew that Herzl wanted to populate his state. In order to gain their support, Herzl was prepared to compromise.

The most obvious way in which he did so was his early decision to concentrate on Palestine as the goal of the movement. Moreover, in his public pronouncements he was prepared to make use of the religious tradition. In his opening speech to the Second Congress he alluded to the biblical claim to Palestine; at the Fourth he spoke of the biblical prophecy of the return. When addressing Wilhelm II in Palestine he was a little more circumspect, denying any property rights to the land, but he still made it clear that Zionism was, despite its modern form, a direct descendant of the Messianic idea. By 1901 his use of the term 'Eretz Israel' shows the extent to which he accepted the religious rationale of the return to Palestine.[54]

In other respects, however, Herzl remained at odds with his own movement. Early on in his diary he wrote that he would work for, not with, the Jews, and this is what in effect he did. His was a very autocratic style of leadership, and he often criticized his supporters for their ungratefulness and pettiness, as well as their sheer inefficiency. At several points in his diary he openly despaired of the members of his movement. Perhaps the most cutting remark was the suggestion for his epitaph: 'He had too good an opinion of the Jews.'[55] He thus never really shook off his negative view of Jews; it re-emerged whenever he received one of his many setbacks.

At one point Herzl described himself as 'the Parnell of the Jews'; this was actually more accurate than he had perhaps intended, for Parnell was the Protestant leader of a largely Catholic nation, an outsider, just as Herzl was the 'Westerner' with the prestige to lead a largely East European Jewish

following. Parnell was an élitist, autocratic, 'modern' nationalist leader, intent on improving as well as liberating his
people, the Irish.[56] Herzl wanted to do the same for the Jews,
if not more so, and ultimately made few concessions to the
cultural tradition of the people whom he had found.

Herzl made repeated exhortations to the Jewish nation to
unite now, and only argue later about the form of the new,
Jewish society.[57] He was also prepared to compromise with
the assimilationists, in order to gain their support.[58] As he
often repeated, his solution was *the* solution precisely because
it satisfied everyone.

Yet Herzl had very firm limits. He was not prepared, for
instance, to compromise the secular, liberal nature of the
movement to satisfy the more orthodox rabbis, those 'of the
blackest colour' as he described them. In his diary he shows
himself willing to allow the traditional kaftan in the new state,
but only if modern hygiene laws are satisfied.[59] In other
words, tradition was all right if it did not get in the way of
modernity. This was also the reason why he rejected Hebrew
as the state language, one of the central demands of cultural
Zionists. As he told S. R. Landau: 'If we create a neo-Hebraic
state, it will end up like modern Greece. If, on the other hand,
we do not shut ourselves up in a language ghetto, the whole
world will belong to us.'[60] Herzl never gave up his vision of
the state of the Jews as a summit of modern civilization, where
Jews could put to good use all that they had learned in exile.
As he said to the Second Congress: 'Yes, we want to return to
our old land. But in the old land we wish a new blossoming of
the Jewish spirit.'[61]

The ambivalences of Herzl in his relation to Jewish tradition come out clearly in his response to Palestine, which he
visited in 1898 on his mission to the German emperor. His
comment in his diary on 'the countryside neglected by the
Arabs', and his equation of the Jewish need for land and the
land's need for development in his address to the emperor,
reveal an essentially colonialist approach to the Holy Land.
Yet this is nothing compared to his response to Jerusalem

itself. 'When I think of you in future, Jerusalem, it shall not be with pleasure,' he wrote. 'The stifling deposits of two thousand years of inhumanity, intolerance, and uncleanliness fester in the evil-smelling alleys. The One Person, the amiable dreamer from Nazareth, who was here all that time, was only able to increase the hatred. If we were ever to get Jerusalem, and I was still around, I would make sure it was first cleaned. I would get rid of everything which was not sacred; build workers' houses outside the city, clear the dirty slums and pull them down. I would burn the ruins which were not holy and put the bazaars somewhere else. Then, while preserving the old building style where possible, I would build a comfortable, well-ventilated new city, with a proper sewage system, around the Holy Places.'

His visit to the Wailing Wall was spoilt for him by all the beggars. He visited the Via Dolorosa, but briefly, because his aides said a Jew should not do this. They also prevented him from visiting Calvary and the Mosque of Omar, the latter because the rabbi of Jerusalem had prohibited visits. Herzl commented: 'How much superstition and fanaticism from all sides.' This was not for a modern, liberal person such as himself.

Yet, on second thoughts, the situation was not perhaps as drastic as he had first thought. His second plan for Jerusalem saw him envisaging leaving the old city as a 'Lourdes and Mecca and Yerushalayim', while a 'very attractive and elegant city' could be built next to it. All the religious and charitable buildings could be put in the old city, while the new city could arise on the (reforested) hills round about. 'With enough care, Jerusalem could be made into a jewel. Everything holy kept within the walls, everything new spread around them.'[62]

The historical, traditional and religious heritage could thus be 'closed within' the walls, to be admired in its picturesque setting, while the new, modern city was left free to expand. If this second version allowed the survival of history intact, instead of its large-scale demolition as in the first version, it nevertheless made tradition effectively safe, so that the modern state could continue unhampered. Despite the revelation of religious tradition, and the Jewish cultural life of East European Jewry, Herzl continued to believe that nothing should be allowed to get in the way of what he had wanted from the start of his campaign: a modern state of the Jews. In the novel *Altneuland* Herzl attempted to show his followers exactly what this meant.

5
ALTNEULAND

Altneuland is the fifth version of Herzl's Zionist idea. In an interview in 1899, he described how he had gone back to working on the novel version of the state of the Jews which he had decided not to write in 1895, in favour of his practical 'book for men'. Now, four years later, the time was right to tell 'the fairytale of the times to come', and to describe the kind of society and living environment which could be constructed from already existing social and technical inventions, if only they were used correctly, or, as he characteristically put it, 'how much justice, goodness and beauty can be created on earth if only there is a decent will to it.'[1]

Herzl's diaries show that he had several ideas for a Zionist novel before he came to write *Altneuland*. When, in the summer of 1895, he was still undecided between the form of a novel or practical plan, he sketched several plot outlines. In one a Hirsch-like character would eventually recognize that a Herzl-like character was right about the need for a state of the Jews. In another an art swindler, having abandoned a woman called Pauline (the name of Herzl's sister), would eventually reclaim his honour and leave for the 'seven-hour land', where workers would sing in choirs and Jewish national 'Passion plays' would be performed. Another brief sketch had a blond hero and a Spanish Jewish heroine, of 'fine race'. Yet another saw Herzl elaborating the basic idea of his Samuel Kohn novel, with the new, Herzl-based hero, now called Moritz Frühlingsfeld, receiving the suicide note from Heinrich (Kana) on the second day of Christmas 1899, leaving the girl behind, and going on a journey to forget.[2]

Almost three years later, in March 1898, the remains of this plot could still be seen in Herzl's idea for a novel about the Viennese press world, which is a coming to terms with his German nationalist past and his journalistic present. The hero would be a Jewish journalist, 'someone like Dr Friedjung', of rabbinic parentage, who becomes very Germanic and undergoes a 'black-red-gold assimilation' as a university fraternity member. Disgusted by the corruption of the press, he sets up his own 'pure' and German paper, with finance from a Jewish entrepreneur. After initial success, the hero suffers from *folie de grandeur* in thinking he can take on Viennese press corruption single-handed, and fails due to his fatal flaw: 'the Germans in Bohemia etc. do not want to be told what to do by a Jew.' He is ultimately disgraced and forced to leave Vienna, leaving the entrepreneur to rescue the newspaper. Yet all is not lost, for the hero has 'discovered Zion', and is consoled by the success of Kadimah, which he had once scorned; he boards ship, perhaps to Palestine, with the 'forgotten girl' as his bride.

Herzl notes details which he wants to include in the story, such as the song of a group of 'neo-Hebrews' which becomes louder as the novel progresses. He wants to have a *Schnorrer* to represent the Jewish *Bohème*; as a contrast he wants to include his new discovery, 'the good, modest, wonderful lower middle class' of Jews. Although the character is based on Heinrich Friedjung there is more than a little touch of the autobiographical about this *Bildungsroman* of a Jewish journalist.[3]

A few days later Herzl thought of a different approach to the question of human development, a drama about Moses. Herzl's Moses is a man who is intent not on a goal, but on the journey, 'education through the journey'. It is also the story of a man who 'is the leader, because he does not want to be', a theme of self-renunciation common in Herzl's self-image, and which reappears in *Altneuland*. 'It is,' adds Herzl, 'the tragedy of the leader, every leader of people, who does not lead people astray.'[4] That it is a tragedy, and that the value of the movement is seen in the movement itself rather than its end, perhaps reflects Herzl's insecurity about the ultimate success of the movement. His attempts to provide a fictional version of Zionism seem indeed to have been the result of those periods when he felt that his practical efforts were going nowhere, and that the only way of preserving the dream, and hope of its realization, was through fiction. As he said at one of these low points in his campaign, in June 1900, he might as well continue writing *Altneuland* as 'our plan is only for novels and the future'. It was the same a few months later: 'I am busy on *Altneuland*. The hopes of practical success have melted away. My life is now no novel. So the novel is now my life.'[5]

Altneuland, the culmination of Herzl's various attempts at a 'Zion novel', was written between 1899 and 1902 to act as a symbol of hope for his followers. As he wrote to the Grand Duke of Baden: 'It is a fairytale, which I tell, as it were, by the campfires, to keep my people in good spirits during the time of wandering. Perseverance is all.' It was also a personal consolation for Herzl, who by 1902 had some regrets that he had not been more serious in pursuing his career as a writer, especially a dramatist.[6] By writing a novel which was a play in disguise, and which also painted a picture of a realizable dream land for the Jews, Herzl satisfied almost all sides of his character, as well as, in his view, creating a powerful piece of propaganda for Zionism at a time when it desperately needed it. *Altneuland* is thus one of the most important documents for understanding Herzl as a Zionist, and Jewish, thinker.

In early August 1899, Herzl wrote in his diary that he wished his testament to the Jewish people to be: 'Make your state so, that the stranger feels at ease among you.'[7] Written at a time when Herzl's ideas for his novel, including the title, were beginning to coalesce, this testament could well serve as the motto of *Altneuland*. It is, in effect, a five-act play on the theme of tolerance.[8] At the same time, it is a much elaborated version of the blueprint provided in *Der Judenstaat*, a hymn to the possibilities for Mankind of technological and social progress, and an attempt to reconcile the German nationalist, the Viennese lawyer and the reborn Jew in Herzl. It is, in other words, a recapitulation of all the strands of his thought which have been traced in these pages. It is also a curious mix between Herzl's new recognitions, and the persistence of his old ideas and goals.

In a *roman à clef* such as this is, where every character has personal and symbolic significance, it is no coincidence that Herzl gives the real hero of the book, and the leader of his new society, the name David Littwak (based on David Wolffsohn). Nor is it accidental that Littwak lives in a house called Friedrichsheim, named after the chorus figure of the book, Friedrich Löwenberg (the young Herzl), but also a tip of the hat to Bismarck's estate at Friedrichsruh.[9] That the Littwaks of this world (the East European Jews) are thus destined to take on the mantle of leadership from Herzl's German idol is confirmed in the plot by the relationship between Herzl's representative of the Old and the New worlds, the Prussian nobleman turned American millionaire Kingscourt (Königshoff), and David Littwak's baby son. Kingscourt, a confirmed misanthrope, is mysteriously attracted to the little Friedrich, the symbol of the Jewish future. He is indeed enthralled, under 'the tyranny of a rosy baby'. Kingscourt goes so far as to let the infant ride him, and so 'he ended up in the funniest sort of slavery.' The Junker thus becomes a slave of love to the Jewish baby, and ultimately stays in Palestine to ensure Friedrich's well-being.[10]

Having thus subordinated the German to the Jew, Herzl also has his Viennese law student, Friedrich Löwenberg, fall in love with David Littwak's sister Mirjam, modelled on his dead sister Pauline. Commentators have pointed out the vaguely incestuous connotations here, but it is also important to point out the symbolic significance of this union of the assimilated, former Viennese law student with a Littwak, with East European Jewry. Löwenberg recognizes the mistake of his former love for the once beautiful but shallow Ernestine Löffler, and cuts his ties with the horrors of Viennese Jewish bourgeois society; instead, in the new Jewish land, he can fulfil himself by marrying Mirjam, the paragon of the new Jewish identity.

This happens as a fitting climax of reconciliation at the

book's end. At the beginning, in Book One, Löwenberg is an 'educated and desperate young man', a typical example of Vienna's unemployed Jewish intelligentsia and the personal embodiment of the best that the Western Jew can be in the context of a thoroughly rotten Viennese Jewish society. Without hope of a successful career, and unlucky in love, he answers an advertisement in the newspaper, and agrees to go with the German-American Kingscourt to a South Sea island. There they will live alone, away from all of despicable humanity—except for their two servants, a mute Negro and a Tahitian.

Kingscourt, a good Mephistopheles, gives Löwenberg 5000 gulden as the price for his company, and Löwenberg, before leaving, gives this to the Littwaks, a poor Jewish family from the East. While sailing through the Mediterranean, Kingscourt suggests that they stop off and have a look at Löwenberg's 'fatherland', Palestine. Löwenberg denies that it is his fatherland, but they do visit the Holy Land, which is decayed, 'like our people', in Löwenberg's words. Kingscourt, on the other hand, is much more optimistic: all it needs is reforestation and water, then it could be a wonderful land, which the Jews should develop.

Book Two starts twenty years later, in 1923, with Kingscourt and Löwenberg sailing back to civilization to see how the world has changed. After hearing that Palestine has become the new commercial centre of the Eastern Mediterranean, they decide to go to Haifa, which, they discover, is now a bustling port and a wonderful, modern city. By pure chance they meet the son of the Jewish peddler to whom Löwenberg had given all his money, David Littwak. The poor Jewish boy has become a successful shipper, and is ecstatic at meeting his benefactor again. He has his Negro servant guard the new visitors' yacht, while he explains to them what has happened in the last two decades, how the Jews 'rescued themselves' from anti-Semitic persecution in Europe.

At lunch, in his villa on Mount Carmel, Littwak explains more about the 'New Society', which is the name for the

Jewish settlement—not so much a state as 'one big co-operative'. He reveals that women now have equal rights, and he describes the workings of the 'Society' and of its extensive welfare system. The party decides to go to a theatre to sample the delights of Jewish high culture. The choice is *Moses* at the National Theatre or *Shabbetai Zvi* at the opera. The latter is chosen. On the way the party stops off to buy the requisite pairs of white gloves at one of the large department stores, which have replaced petty traders. Book One ends at the opera, the symbol of how civilized the state of the Jews can be.

Book Three, 'The blooming land', starts with a journey through the new, fertile countryside, with artisans' houses and carefully tended fields, where fruit and produce is grown for export 'to all parts of the world'. The Arabs, it is explained, have welcomed the prosperity brought by the Jews. If anyone is a source of trouble, it is not the tolerant Muslims but rather pseudo-orthodox troublemakers such as Dr Geyer, who is trying to appeal to the masses through a selfish form of nationalism. This becomes evident on a visit to the co-operative farm of Neudorf, where Littwak and Steineck are campaigning for their political party against the narrow nationalism of Geyer's supporters. At the electoral meeting Littwak saves the day for liberalism through his rhetorical brilliance, and his ability to sway the masses.

The party then travels on to the Sea of Galilee, which is just like the Riviera. The medical research institute of the bacteriologist Steineck is visited, where the doctor is searching for a cure for malaria to open up Africa to civilization. Book Three ends with a conversation in a spa garden where Löwenberg's former Viennese acquaintances explain that, with the Jewish homeland, now Jews can live at peace in Europe as well. Indeed only now has the full emancipation been achieved there. Either Jews have assimilated, or they are respected as Jews, as members of another state: because the Jews treat their minorities well, they are treated well as a minority elsewhere. 'For tolerance can and will always only rest on reciprocity.'[11]

Book Four, 'Pesach', is dominated by the account by Jo Levy (alias Joseph Cowen) of how the modern exodus was achieved. This, Herzl's blueprint for the Zionist strategy, is introduced as the modern accompaniment to the Seder: after the traditional meal and ritual, Levy's account is played to the Seder participants on a most modern instrument: the phonograph. As Littwak remarks: 'The old wants to transform itself into the new.' Jews, having become 'new people' while remaining 'true to their roots', now sit and listen, in an atmosphere of reverence, to the modern story of their deliverance. After this, Mirjam, Littwak's sister, explains to Löwenberg the system of international education for Jewish children; a model open prison is visited; and the party tours the flourishing Jordan Valley, travelling to the spa town of Jericho. Book Four ends with a heroic description of the workings of the Dead Sea Canal and its hydro-electric turbines.

Book Five, the culmination of the journey from Vienna, takes place in Jerusalem. The new city is the one Herzl had imagined back in 1898, all modern and spacious. The old city has remained much the same, except for the new palace of peace and the rebuilt Temple. The palace of peace is a forum in which the remaining problems of the world can be discussed. The nations of the world elect a council which administers the peace palace's funds for natural disasters. Above the portal of the palace is the motto: 'Nil humani a me alienum puto'.[12] The Temple, on the other hand, 'was rebuilt, because the fullness of time had come'. At the moment of his own fulfilment, Löwenberg, listening to the song to the Sabbath bride, thinks of Heine, of the German poet's pride in his Jewish identity, and then of the horrible self-abasement of his former Viennese Jewish contemporaries, whose self-contempt as Jews led to their being held in contempt and hated by everyone else.

Now, Löwenberg recognizes, the Jews have rescued themselves and regained their pride. The rebuilt Temple is only a symbol for something else, something invisible: 'For only here had they achieved the free community, in which they could work for the highest goals of humanity.' Jews had known real community earlier, but without freedom. They had known freedom, when the civilized nations had given them equal rights, but then they had ceased to be Jews. 'Both had to be there: freedom and the feeling of community.' Only now could they build a temple to the invisible and Almighty 'who is present throughout the universe as the will to good.'[13]

This is the emotional climax of the book. From here on, there is a visit to a Jewish artist's atelier, so that Herzl can describe the workings of the Jewish Academy. It also gives Mirjam an opportunity to sing the songs of, among others, Wagner. Later, seated in a railway carriage, Kingscourt and Löwenberg discuss the possibilities of the new mutualist approach to social organization, and how it is to be achieved.

The book's finale is the election of David Littwak as president of the new society, despite his reluctance to be the leader. He ultimately only accepts because his father tells him it will make his dying mother happy, a very Herzlian solution. There is then a final recapitulation of how the new society was made possible, in which all the main characters answer Löwenberg's question in their own way, and Herzl gives us his recipe for success: need, the reunited people, the new forms of transport, science, the will, the forces of nature, mutual tolerance, self-confidence, love and suffering, and God.

Into the framework of this plot, Herzl weaves all the main aspects of his Zionist ideology, diagnosis of the Jewish problem, his proposed remedy, and the ideals which he thinks that remedy can realize. By setting the first part of the book in turn of the century Vienna, Herzl makes his own experience of the Jewish problem paradigmatic for the problem in general. Here, in the opening pages of *Altneuland*, is a picture of the corrupt, and corrupting, nature of Viennese Jewish society which has changed hardly at all from that of the pre-Zionist Herzl. The parvenu Jews in the Löffler salon are shallow, cynical, and only interested in money and luxury.

They are, furthermore, ashamed of being Jewish. The young Jewish intelligentsia, the victims in Herzl's eyes of the ideology of emancipation, are little better. Many of them have corrupted the world of the liberal professions and academia by transferring to that world the business ethics of their fathers, which are quite unsuitable to it. Admittedly these young Jews were in effect forced to do so, due to the over-competition in these sectors, but that does not lessen the fact of their negative impact on professional morals.

Marriage has also been reduced in this Jewish bourgeois world to a matter of money and business connections, as is made plain by Ernestine Löffler's betrothal to the unprepossessing Leopold Weinberger. In describing this figure, with a bald pate, a squint and sweaty hands, Herzl comes very close to anti-Semitic caricature. Indeed his general description of the Viennese Jewish bourgeoisie could be mistaken for anti-Semitic propaganda.

There are, of course, good Jews, such as Friedrich Löwenberg. Anti-Semitism, however, makes it impossible for such people to have the Christian contacts necessary to end their dependence on the new ghetto. Similarly, anti-Semitism is making life impossible for the poor Jewish immigrants, such as the Littwaks, whose moral rectitude clearly makes them deserving of a better fate, and help from above. The rich Jews, whose craven imitation of non-Jewish society and contempt for their own Jewishness are largely to blame for anti-Semitism (as Herzl later spells out for us), think that contributing to charitable organizations is enough to aid their poor brethren, and try to ignore the problems caused by anti-Semitism, hiding behind the protection of the state's police—a sad state of affairs, as Herzl has a rabbi point out. The Jews of the Löffler salon try to laugh off their predicament, but even there premonitions abound that 'we shall soon have to wear the yellow badge.'[14]

Having given us this diagnosis, Herzl then gives us his remedy. Things will get so bad, he predicts, that the Jews will eventually see the wisdom of Zionism, and 'rescue ourselves'.

This involves two things: the moral decision of Jews to unite in the national revival, and the political and logistical problems of setting up a new state. On the first point, Herzl more than hints that it is up to Jews to summon up the willpower and self-respect to solve the Jewish problem. This, after all, is the premise of the whole book: 'If you will it, it is no fairytale.' There are also occasions when it is made clear that, if only Jews stood up to their oppressors, they would gain respect, and so lessen anti-Semitism. People's attitudes to the Jews cannot be changed by decree, but only by what the Jews themselves do. As Kingscourt is made to say, 'one cannot abolish prejudices, so one must conquer them for oneself.'[15] The action Jews should take is to join together in setting up their own national society: Zionism. Jews cannot wait for miracles to happen, as in the days of Shabbetai Zvi; today they must unite and redeem themselves. David Littwak's remarks on Shabbetai Zvi show Herzl asserting that the people of Israel is its own Messiah.[16]

Once the Jews have gained national consciousness, the practical steps will follow, and these are outlined in the account by Jo Levy in Book Four.[17] By now, Herzl was not even insisting on having full sovereignty for the Jewish homeland, for he has Levy sign a treaty with the Ottomans whereby the Jews pay a large sum for the right of self-government and colonization in a large Palestine, while the Sultan retains ultimate sovereignty. The colonization is financed by the united Jewish charities and a loan organized by the 'New Society for the Colonization of Palestine', and is overseen by the Congress. Herzl envisages Levy, based in London, directing the as yet secret preparations for the mass colonization. The realization of this is then described in a large amount of logistical detail, as if to assure the reader that this is indeed 'no fairytale'.

What marks Herzl's description of the colonization, and indeed of the new colony, is his use of technological and social advance to make his argument for him. Typical of this is his having Levy tell how the problem of having no draught animals in the new land was solved by importing hundreds of 'electric ploughs', which could be powered by electricity stations fired by coal imported from England. This technological revolution is then itself revolutionized by the construction of hydro-electric stations to replace the need for coal. The 'new Chad-Gadya' (oxen replaced by coal, replaced by hydro-electric power) is only one of many instances of Herzl trying to explore the possibilities of modern man. Kingscourt explains the rationale of Herzl's technological vision while sailing through the Red Sea. Moses, he says, would not understand the 'miracles' of modern technology, but he would laugh at the misuse humanity makes of it. The pity is that all the world's problems could be solved today, if only people were sensible: 'With the ideas, knowledge, and means which is at humanity's disposal today, on 31 December 1902, there should be no problems. One does not need a philosopher's stone, or a guided aircraft. Everything needed to make a better world is already available. And, my friend, do you know who could show the way forward? You! You Jews! Precisely because you are in such dire straits; you have nothing to lose. You could create the experimental land for humanity—over there, where we were, create a new land on the old soil. Old-newland!'[18]

This is exactly what Herzl has the Jews in Old-newland do. Everything he describes in terms of technology was already available when he published the book in 1902, was, in other words, realistic. What makes the new land seem spectacular is the imaginative and enterprising use made of such advances as the electric train and the telephone. For a book written around 1900, Herzl's technological and economic vision is impressive. There are electric street lamps everywhere, automobiles, an electric monorail in Haifa, and this modern city is not crowded but rather spacious, with single family houses forming a sea around large department stores and public buildings. Electricity has spread out industry, so that artisans can work in the countryside again. At the Dead Sea there are chemical industries, while the Dead Sea Canal, a system of underground tunnels from the Mediterranean to the Dead Sea, provides hydro-electric power, and replenishes the level of the inland sea, to make up for the water taken out to irrigate the now flourishing Jordan Valley. 'The real founders of Old-newland,' Herzl has Littwak say, 'were the hydro-technicians.'[19] The country is further covered with a rail network, with electric trains of course, which not only unites the whole land, but also links it up to Europe, by way of the Berlin to Baghdad Railway, and Africa, by way of the Cape to Cairo (now Jerusalem) Railway. Old-newland is actually at the crux of the Old World's commercial (rail) routes. Some of this is rather far-fetched, but most is surprisingly accurate. There is even the idea of a telephone news service, with advertisements which are much more expensive than those in newspapers, because on the 'phone (radio) the advertisements cannot be ignored. All of this technological vision shows Herzl's deep faith in the power of technology to overcome Man's problems. It is thus very much in character that he has Steineck propose a commemoration in 1925, by three toots on the whistles of all the world's trains, of Robert Stephenson's Stockton to Darlington Railway. Stephenson, after all, was 'the bringer of the new age'.[20]

What Herzl also does here is show how the state of the Jews can take all that is most modern and best in Europe and America, as Kingscourt had said. Thus the Jewish cities are built following principles borrowed from the Americans; the children are taught English sports such as cricket, football and tennis; there are English and Swiss hotels; and continental-style spas. While in the new city of Jerusalem, walking through an English-style park, past a German-style health office, Kingscourt says to Löwenberg: 'I now understand everything in Old-newland. It is a mosaic—a Mosaic mosaic.'[21] It is an amalgam of Europe and America, only better.

What is more, the Jews are introducing these progressive ideas into the Orient, and, Herzl is predicting, the material benefits which will accrue from this importation of progress and technological know-how will make the Jews loved by their neighbours. Jewish breakthroughs in medical research are going to be particularly well received. Thus the Eichenstamms' ophthalmological institute in Jerusalem has become a beacon of light throughout North Africa and Asia for those threatened with blindness. Sascha Eichenstamm proudly states: 'The blessings which have ushered forth like a stream from our medical institutes have made us more friends here in Palestine and the neighbouring lands than all of our technical and industrial plants.'[22] The bacteriologist Steineck is trying to make the whole world grateful to the Jews. He is searching for a cure for malaria, to make Africa safe for colonization by the surplus population of Europe. Indeed the blacks of America will also be able then to 'go home', and thus the 'Negro problem' in America will be solved just as the Jewish problem was. And everyone will thank the Jews for it.[23]

As a complement to this technological and scientific sophistication, Herzl envisaged a social system which would be the most progressive imaginable. Herzl was very sensitive to the connection between technology and society. His idea that electricity would solve the problem of socialism, by dispersing the teeming masses from the cities where they had been concentrated by steam power, is quite prescient. His social vision in *Altneuland* is based on a similar, if less accurate, perception. At an automobile exhibition in Paris in 1900 he saw an American exhibit, the 'Cleveland car', which was powered by batteries and had a range of 100 kilometres. He saw that these kinds of cars would need an extensive network of battery replacement stations, and he also thought that these could be provided by a suitably modern form of social and economic interaction, a co-operative system of car owners. He continued: 'Between capitalism and collectivism, mutualism appears to me to be the middle way. The producer and consumer co-operatives are only the beginnings, the premonitions of the mutual principle.'[24] Herzl was plainly sold on this idea, which a fellow Zionist, Franz Oppenheimer, was doing much to develop.[25] 'Mutualism' is indeed what he proposes for his model society of the future.

Altneuland is full of the economic and social voluntary associations which characterize Herzl's mutualist society. Newspapers, Herzl's pet subject, are owned by their readerships. The opera is owned by its subscribers, as is the telephone service. Agriculture, as typified by the settlement of Neudorf, is organized into a system of proto-kibbutz co-operative farms. Grocery stores are organized by consumer co-operatives, so there are few individual traders. Even where the mutual principle was at first unsuitable, as in shipping, the source of Littwak's new wealth, the enlightened employer is in the process of selling his firm to his workers. The whole society, the New Society, is indeed one big voluntary association. Membership is not automatic; it has to be earned by two years of service to the community. That said, it is open to all, Jew and non-Jew alike, and has many benefits, including free education for all and an extensive welfare system (made possible by the institution of the two-year service to the community). It is a quasi-Fabian dream.

This mutualist social vision is based on the two major aspects of Herzl's thought. On the one hand it is clearly Herzl's anticipation of the future trends of society, and his stated wish to utilize what was already present as well as possible. Thus there is a great reliance on statistics and planning to provide 'a freedom without crazy over-production'.[26] Here Herzl cites the example of military organization, and reveals his technocratic confidence that statistical and managerial techniques could free men from being slaves to the market. Similarly, his new society is provided with its goods not by petty traders and hawkers but by mammoth department stores, using economies of scale to outbid the little man. Around 1900 the department store did indeed seem to be the retailing form of the future, so, as Herzl has Littwak explain, the New Society decides to have department stores from the start, so that petty trade, the bane of Jewish life in Europe, is prevented by its modern equivalent. Instead of having to cope with the pain of economic readjustment and the unwelcome aspects of the old, 'we started immediately with modernity.'[27] Next to the department store, the co-operative and the cartel (trust) seemed the economic forms of the future. Therefore, as Herzl has Löwenberg say, it is not surprising that the end result would be a 'cartel of co-operatives'. Herzl thus takes the oligopolistic trends of late nineteenth-century capitalism, especially in Germany, and gives them a progressive, quasi-democratic gloss.

If Herzl was anticipating trends in his adoption of mutualism, he was, on the other hand, also convinced that this was the solution to the social problem which he had sought even before becoming a Zionist. His central question was one asked by many social and political thinkers at the turn of the century: how could a society be created which was fair without coercion and free without economic and social injustice? It was particularly important from Herzl's perspective to find this middle way between socialism and capitalism, for two related reasons.

The first of these was Herzl's background in German social thought, especially in its Hegelian and nationalist varieties. Through his law professors, Lorenz von Stein and Anton Menger, Herzl would have learnt of the need for an active role of the state in pursuit of social justice. Stein was also one of the major influences on those of Herzl's contemporaries, such as Victor Adler and Heinrich Friedjung, who became German nationalists in the 1870s because they saw the nation as the proper vehicle to achieve the social justice which *laissez faire* liberalism was neglecting. There was a similar connection between nationalism and social justice in the thought of one of Herzl's role models, Ferdinand Lassalle, a Jew, a leader of German socialism, and an ardent German patriot, who saw the nation-state as the proper focus of socialist endeavour. Herzl clearly was also inspired by English and French thought on the matter, but the main influences would appear to have come from Germany and Austria, with Bismarck's 'state socialism' being another important factor. It is not, I think, accidental, that Herzl sees one major justification for his cartel of co-operatives being the resulting social and economic security which this would provide.[28]

There was, however, another major reason for Herzl's concern in finding this middle way, which was also related to his German nationalist background, and this was his perception of the place of Jews in society. As we have seen, his diagnosis of the Jewish problem had been that in an anti-Semitic society the Jews were condemned to be at both extremes, both capitalists and socialists, and so be doubly exposed to attack. It is thus as a solution not only to the social, but also to the Jewish problem that: 'In our society the individual is neither crushed between the grinding wheels of capitalism, nor beheaded by socialist levelling.'[29]

What Herzl essentially means by this is that, by using the co-operative system, planning, and modern forms such as the department stores, all the evils of capitalism (and hence Jewish life) can be avoided, and the good aspects, individual liberty and the right to private property, preserved. There are Jewish artisans and Jewish farmers; there are no Jewish peddlars. This is the realization of Herzl's idea, already seen in *Der Judenstaat*, that by creating a new society from a *tabula rasa* the Jews could avoid the burdens of the past and provide Europe with a model of what was possible in modernity. Herzl uses a most interesting term to describe this freedom from the past: 'We have, as it were, created our society without hereditary affliction.'[30] One's origins, the past, do not count any more; in this situation the just society is possible in a way in which it was not in a Europe where inheritance—and heredity—was all.

Herzl's new society attempts to be both liberal and patriarchal at the same time. It is intent on directing people to be free. Littwak has thus encouraged his workers to buy his company from him, as he knows what is best for them: 'It is, if you like, the patriarchal relationship, but in a modern commercial form.'[31] This commercial patriarchalism is matched by a matriarchal welfare system, whereby the women in the New Society exercise their equal rights and status by managing the comprehensive welfare system, which guarantees, as well as the usual areas of charitable concern, the right to work. The obverse of this is that begging is explicitly banned in this liberal society. Individual rights are actually subject to major limitations. No New Society member is allowed to own land. All land is held on a jubilee (fifty-year) leasehold, after which it reverts to the New Society. This is to ensure that no unfair advantage accrues from inherited wealth. There is a similar logic in education, where a lavishly organized system is free to all, and equality is ensured by the compulsory wearing of uniforms. There would therefore seem to be no room for private education, for this would jeopardize Herzl's carefully constructed system, which, while it allows for disparities in wealth to create incentives, is intent on producing complete equality of opportunity. The rights of individuals are thus curtailed to ensure that 'hereditary affliction' never applies to the state of the Jews.

This is apparently an illiberal policy on Herzl's part, but, if it is, it is one many liberals might have made when trying to counter the effect of history on social development. Herzl's state of the Jews is, in fact, so 'liberal' in this version that it ceases to be a state at all. Although its welfare system is organized like the Austro-Hungarian army, and there is the hint of an informal militia, the New Society has no military. There must be a coercive force of some sort, given the model prison we are shown, yet none is actually apparent in society. Instead it is a 'free community', completely dependent on the voluntary adherence of its members to the association's laws. In this way Herzl reverses his previous position: the gestor of the Society of Jews, in effect, has turned itself into the ideal Rousseauesque contractual state, which is entirely based on voluntary adherence.

To most commentators this non-state state has appeared an outlandish invention on Herzl's part, quite belying his claims to practicality. It has also been characterized as a borrowing from anarchism, which Herzl encountered while in Paris. From Herzl's perspective it might not have appeared so impractical or anarchic. He does, after all, point to the United States as an example of a society with very little outward sign of state regulation, and it might be added that the liberal state of his time, most notably England, had remarkably little control over its populace.[32] In terms of the roots of the idea of society as a voluntary association, Herzl explicitly calls on the biblical example of the time when every man will sit in peace under his vine and his fig tree. There is, however, another parallel which Herzl does not explicitly mention, but which may well be of relevance, that of the associations of educated individuals, the *Vereine* of *Gebildeten*, which typified early nineteenth-century German liberal social life. The ideologically loaded form of the *Verein* later became the main building block not only of German liberal organization, but also that of Jewish emancipationists. In making his model society an association of voluntary associations, Herzl was also, perhaps unconsciously, mimicking the ideology of emancipation.[33]

The New Society is, as has been mentioned, open to all. In the novel at least two non-Jews are, or become, members: Kingscourt and a Palestinian Arab, Reschid Bey. It is through Bey that Herzl answers the question which has only grown in relevance since: how is such a Jewish homeland possible when there are already inhabitants there? Herzl has Kingscourt ask the pertinent question about the impact of the Jewish settlement on the native population while the party is travelling through the reborn Palestinian countryside. The answer, given the technological, agricultural and social miracles which have been achieved, is not all that surprising. Bey replies: 'For us all it was a blessing.' This is because the native landowners have profited from higher land prices, and the landless Arab workers have gained regular employment, and, whether they liked it or not, the benefits of the sophisticated new welfare system. The general development of the land has also made their lives, as well as those of the Jewish settlers, better, without their having to sacrifice their culture in return. Asked by Kingscourt whether the Jews were not, even so, resented as 'interlopers', Reschid Bey replies: 'Would you think of someone as a robber, who does not take anything from you, but rather brings you something? The Jews have made us prosperous, why should we be angry with them? They live with us as brothers, why should we not love them?'[34] The material and social benefits of progressive and humane civilization have thus, rather ingenuously, won the day. One has to remember how pessimistic Herzl was about Europe, and also America, to realize just how much wishful thinking has gone into this argument that prosperity will make the Jews welcome.

By making the New Society open to all Herzl answered another question which has dogged the Zionist project, and Israel: whether it is an exclusivist, racist national movement and state. Clearly, and centrally, Herzl's state is inclusivist and non-racial. Yet much of the criticism of *Altneuland* in Zionist ranks was precisely on this point. If the Jewish homeland is open to all, Jews and non-Jews alike, then what, if anything, is Jewish about it? These Zionist critics, and especially the cultural Zionists, could also point to the fact that there is, indeed, little that is specifically Jewish in the character, form and substance of Old-newland. Not only was it not only for Jews, it was not Jewish. At first sight this seems clear, and is a result of Herzl's continued wish to reform the Jews. Yet, on closer inspection, one can discern a very strong Jewish theme, albeit one which identifies Herzl as an heir to the Central European, and not Eastern European, modern Jewish tradition.

Herzl's aim in *Altneuland* is still to reform the Jews. Ironically, the Viennese Jews whom Löwenberg despised at the start of the book continue to be despicable in the new land. They refuse to join the New Society, and as a result are still inwardly not free. As Schiffmann, a repentant Viennese, says: 'We are still standing and looking out between the bars, to where the free people are.' The Viennese are still in their 'ape cage'.[35] If Herzl thus vents his spleen on his rejection by the Viennese establishment, he is also confident that, although some Jews are, in this and similar ways, unreformed, what

counts is that they are now the exceptions. Most Jews in their
own land are upright, hard-working citizens. Begging has
been banned, and there are hardly any Jewish petty traders:
what peddlars there are are Armenians, Greeks and the like,
very few Jews. There is no mention of a stock exchange in the
New Society.

The new Jewish identity is provided by David Littwak and
his sister Mirjam, who are both very proud of their Jewish
heritage, and very conscientious members of the Society. At
the same time, they are extremely refined, very tolerant, and
speak German, which is the main language in the country.
One of the signs, indeed, of the Jewish achievement is that
Mirjam can speak with confidence and ease with an English
noblewoman. As Löwenberg comments: 'now we can even
manage a modest appearance in society.'[36] The East European
Jews have thus managed the successful acculturation to the
norms of civilized society which were beyond their snobbish
Viennese counterparts. Yet there is little explicitly Jewish in
this politeness and refinement.

Religion does have a prominent place in the book, whether
it be in the description of the Passover ceremony, or in the
visit to the rebuilt Temple. Herzl also makes clear through
Löwenberg's reactions the emotional impact which religion
had on him personally. Yet, just as the old city of Jerusalem is
cherished in a cleaned-up version while modernity proceeds
around it, so religion, while respected, is clearly excluded
from having any influence on public life.[37] The defeat of the
Tartuffian Orthodox Rabbi Geyer confirms the fact that
there is complete freedom for all religions, indeed for all
nationalities. As for Hebrew, that is fine as a religious language, and a language of ceremonial songs. It seems to have
no place as a language of everyday life.

Despite this lack of an obvious Jewish identity, Herzl's
vision is very Jewish, in his own terms. Herzl has the architect
Steineck scoff at the idea of the Jewish mission, but this cannot
mask the fact that what Herzl's society represents is the
embodiment of that Jewish mission, only in a national, not

individual, form. What is Jewish about the New Society for Herzl is that it is a model of tolerance, freedom and humanity; it is the achievement of what the emancipation tried, and failed, to do in Europe. This is clear in the central part of the book, where the question of tolerance receives its fullest discussion, in the debate at an electoral meeting in Neudorf between the tolerant, inclusivist liberals such as Littwak and Steineck, on the one hand, and the exclusivist, nationalist supporters of the demagogue and charlatan Geyer, on the other. The central question is clear: should the 'new society' only be for Jews, the people who achieved its prosperity, or should it remain open to all who are prepared to devote two years of their lives to its service? Steineck puts the case too brusquely, too straightforwardly: 'you should hold on to what made us great, liberality, tolerance and love of Mankind. Only then is Zion Zion!' Littwak, in a speech which reads almost as a model Herzlian speech to the masses, and which, intentionally I think, is at the very centre of the book, gives a more persuasive rendering of the same idea.

Littwak points out that the farmers at Neudorf did the work which created prosperity, but the success of their community, and of the 'new society', depends on the 'experiences, books and dreams' of others. Utopian thinkers such as Fourier, Bellamy and Hertzka contributed much, despite their illusions. The English did most, along with the Germans, in developing the co-operative idea. Then there was the Rahaline experiment in Ireland, which was the basis of the Neudorf farming community and the thousands like it. In other words, if Jews had the strength to realize the new society, because they were driven to it by persecution, they also could only do so because 'we are standing on the shoulders of other civilized peoples.' Now Jews should not turn away others, who in any case will only help make the land prosper more. To the applause of all he concludes: 'But all the food you plant is worth nothing, and will rot, if liberality, generosity and love of Mankind do not prosper amongst you.' The 'new society' is thus for the general benefit of humanity, as Herzl had all along dreamed.'[38]

The openness of the state of the Jews was something which meant a great deal to Herzl. Just as he advised Chamberlain in 1903 that, 'for England's glory', English liberality concerning immigration should not be curtailed, so for his own state he wanted it to be true to its own historical mission of being a symbol of tolerance and humanity.[39] The example of Steineck's plan for the opening up of Africa, with its 'solution of the Negro problem', unfortunate though it might appear to us today, shows Herzl envisaging a Jewish people contributing mightily to the well-being of Mankind. In this sense the tolerance of the stranger, which Herzl makes the epitaph of the dead president Eichenstamm,[40] as he once proposed for himself, is part of a general openness to the rest of the world. Zionism is not the segregation of the Jews from the world, but their true integration into it.

Nowhere is this international dimension made so clear as in a peculiar episode in Levy's account of the colonization. Levy recounts how, in the midst of the 'conquest' of the land, he arranged for 500 of the world's intellectual élite to sail to Palestine aboard the ship *Futuro*, where a 'new Platonic dialogue' resulted. The purpose behind the trip was ostensibly for Levy to use the ideas which emerged from the ship's passengers as a result of their experience of Palestine. Yet there is another, very Herzlian reason: the world's respect, recognition and approval of the state of the Jews. The *Futuro* is clearly a forum of the world's judgement: 'And every 25 years a *Futuro* steamer should bring such an Areopagus[41] to us, to whose judgement we shall submit,' Levy proclaims. 'We will not build the Potemkin villages of a world exhibition. The whole land should be open to inspection, the guests of the *Futuro* our worthy jury.'[42]

If the Jews are going to submit themselves to the world's judgement, they are also going to be always at the centre of world attention. The peace palace and the rebuilt Temple are two sides of the same coin. If *Altneuland* is centred on the idea of tolerance, it culminates with the expression of the interdependence of the national and the international community. Jerusalem is both a national and international centre. If the Temple symbolizes the achievement by Jews of a 'free community', then that 'free community' is there to achieve 'the highest goals of humanity'. The Jewish Academy, one of the expressions of the Jews' new 'free community', is explicitly there to embody the Jewish commitment to Mankind in general. In its very composition it symbolizes the Jewish mission to unite the world: 'It naturally transpired that the forty Jews of the Academy were free of national chauvinism. When the institution was founded, its first members came from many linguistically different cultures, and they united on the basis of humanity.' The first clause in the academy's charter states that it has 'the task to seek out the contributions of individuals to humanity'.[43] Humanity, not Judaism or Jewry.

Does this not prove that the state of the Jews is indeed not Jewish, without any Jewish character? Not really, for it is in effect Herzl's liberal-national version of the Central European interpretation of the Jewish mission, that the Jews are to be 'a light unto the nations'.

It is true that Herzl ascribes hardly any of the values of the new state to Jewish tradition itself. The central theme of the book is that Jewish tolerance of others is in return for, and as a result of, the Western values taught to the Jews; it is not derived from Jewish values as such. Yet if Herzl sees the Jews as indebted to Western civilization for the cosmopolitan values which they now espouse as their own, his 'world-historical' vision also sees the expression of these Western values as the new Jewish mission to the world. Old-newland, with its technological, economic, scientific and social achievements, its adherence to the principles of tolerance, justice and freedom, especially religious freedom, is Herzl's vision of the full realization of the Jewish ideology of emancipation. Indeed what is Jewish about the new land is precisely its striving for, and achievement of, that emancipation.

There is a final irony in Herzl's vision. If Old-newland is

the culmination of Jewish emancipation, it is also plainly a model for the rest of the world to emulate. Palestine is not on the edge of the civilized world; it is now at the centre of world commerce, of world culture, and of world politics (hence the peace palace). If Old-newland is not 'Jewish' in the sense that Herzl's critics wished, the reason is that the Jews have not only fully integrated into the world, they have become its very centre.

6

STRUGGLE FOR THE FUTURE

Altneuland was Herzl's ideal vision of the Jewish future. It was, as will have become plain, the culmination of his thinking on the Jewish problem, extending back to before his discovery of Zionism. His final idea, that the Jews could create, if only they willed it, the model society of humanity, economically advanced, socially just and a paragon of liberty and tolerance, was a genuinely felt 'dream', with its roots in the liberal Jewish tradition in which he had been raised. Zionism was, for Herzl, more than just a political solution to the Jewish problem, it had become an ethical ideal as well. As he himself said: 'in Zionism, as I understand it, there is not only the striving for a legally secured soil for our poor people; there is the striving for moral and spiritual perfection.'[1] *Altneuland* was Herzl's sincere vision of the way to realize this goal.

The extent of misunderstanding and criticism to which the book was subjected by his fellow Zionists, especially the 'cultural Zionists', revealed how little Herzl had been able to reconcile his views with those of the Easterners, or, obversely, how unsuccessful had been his attempts to impose his vision on the movement of which he was the leader. Buber once said, 'we venerated him, loved him, but a great part of his being was alien to our soul.'[2] He was right. The very idea of 'our soul' was one Herzl would have found difficult to accept. Despite his German nationalist sympathies, he was never really as devoted to Romantic ideas about national essences, and certainly not a Jewish national essence, as were figures such as Buber and Ahad Ha'am. Instead his ideas stemmed from an Enlightened, liberal tradition.

Usually the clash between Herzl and his cultural Zionist opponents is seen as one between 'West' and 'East', but this is not strictly accurate. The real clash was between the specifically Central European emancipatory tradition from which Herzl came, with its strongly universalistic interpretation of Judaism, and the more particularistic approach of the Jews from the Russian Pale and Galicia, who found a Romantic model for their thought more suited to their ends. When, for instance, someone such as Martin Buber used the German word 'Kultur' (culture) he meant something organic, from the roots of the nation, whether it be German, Jewish or whatever. Herzl, on the other hand, plainly uses 'Kultur' in his diaries in the way we would use 'civilization', that is to say a general, universal concept, applicable to all 'progress', especially technological, regardless of national identity. What the reaction to *Altneuland* shows, and what lay behind the Uganda crisis, was the fact that what Herzl understood by Jewishness, and what his opponents understood by it, were as chalk and cheese: both the products of modernity, but from quite different Jewish traditions.

The attack against Herzl's blueprint of the Zionist future was led, notoriously, by Ahad Ha'am. The latter's critique is, from a cultural Zionist's point of view, devastating. He pointed out the complete lack of any properly Jewish identity in the book. The Jewish Academy was devoted to general human questions, not to Jewish ones. Unlike the French Academy, on which it was supposedly based and which was notoriously concerned about the French language, the Jewish Academy did not even speak Hebrew. Indeed the language question, and Hebrew in particular, was almost completely ignored. In order to please the non-Jews and anti-Semites, Ahad Ha'am charged, Herzl had put an excessive emphasis on the principle of tolerance, and the debt that the new state would have to European civilization. The leading idea of the book was summed up by the phrase 'without distinction of nationality or religion', even though this was supposed to be a Jewish society.

Then again, there were practical problems. It was fantasy to think that the millions of world Jewry could be resettled in the space of twenty years. And what about the Arabs? Here Ahad Ha'am pointed out, as he had done back in 1891 after his trip to Palestine, what was to be a fatal flaw in the Herzlian version of Zionism: 'Peace and brotherly love reign between them and the Jews, who took nothing from them and gave them so much. A delightful idyll, indeed. Only, it is not quite clear how the New Society managed to obtain sufficient land for the millions of Jews from all over the world if all the arable land previously in Arab hands, i.e. most of the arable land in Palestine altogether, continues to remain in their hands as before.' Ahad Ha'am further attacked Herzl's dream of rebuilding the Temple, one of the author's most obvious attempts at creating a Jewish identity for the new land, and, as we have seen, the symbol of the summit of his wishes. Not only did he scoff at the rebuilt Temple as a glorified Viennese synagogue, with its organ music; he also, acutely, asked where it was to be built. Surely not where the Mosque of Omar now stood? Yet where else was religiously acceptable?

It was Herzl's pandering to Western civilization, however, to which Ahad Ha'am truly objected. He picked up on the unfortunate episode in the book about solving the American Negro problem, by pointing out that the new Negro movement's ideal, if based on the same premisses as Herzl's Zionism, would be virtually identical to *Altneuland*. 'To copy others without showing a spark of original talent; to avoid "national chauvinism" in such fashion as to leave no trace of the character of one's own people or of its literature and spiritual creations; to gather oneself together and retreat into a corner merely to show others that we are tolerant, tolerant to the point of wearisomeness—that can be done by the Negroes too. And yet, who knows, perhaps they too would be incapable of such a performance.' In other words, the

Negroes would not be able to sink as low as Herzl in exempli-
fying the 'slavery within freedom' so typical of Western
thought.[3]

From his own perspective Ahad Ha'am was quite correct
about *Altneuland*, as we have seen. Yet from Herzl's perspective, and that of supporters such as Nordau, this critique
smacked of exclusivism, mysticism and, indeed, reactionism.
It completely missed the point of the Jews being at the
forefront of history, the most modern and most liberal of
peoples, leading the other nations of the world on to a
millennium of pure humanity, which was Herzl's vision, as it
had been that of the liberal, reform tradition of Central
European Jewry before him. To Herzl this vision of a pure
humanity was Jewish, to Ahad Ha'am it was flight from the
national spirit. The two views were almost completely ir-
reconcilable, as they have remained to this day.

It was thus not merely as a response to the personal attack
on his leadership that Herzl had his lieutenant, Max Nordau,
launch a counterattack on Ahad Ha'am. There was this other
consideration, that Ahad Ha'am's criticism was also an attack
on Herzl's whole liberal and modern 'dream' for the Jewish
people. That said, Nordau's eventual riposte was quite excessive. He accused the spiritual father of cultural Zionism of
being against the principle of tolerance, and wanting to
impose Russian values on the new society: 'the only thing he
wants to take with him to Altneuland are the guidelines of the
Inquisition, the customs of the anti-Semites, and the anti-
Jewish laws of Russia.' Moreover, Ahad Ha'am, though he
wrote good Hebrew, had nothing to say in it. He was, in
effect, a 'secular protest rabbi', and anti-Zionist.

This vicious attack appalled not only the cultural Zionists,
for good reason. If Ahad Ha'am opposed Herzl's version of
the state of the Jews, this was not because he wished the Jewish
state to be intolerant and reactionary, as Nordau accused. Far
from it, in many ways Ahad Ha'am's vision of the Jewish state
as a beacon of Jewish culture to a world Jewish community
still living largely in the Diaspora was far more practical

(because politically more modest), humane and ethically founded than Herzl's emancipatory dream. It was, after all, Ahad Ha'am and not Herzl who insisted on proper consideration of the Arab population of Palestine. To accuse Ahad Ha'am as Nordau did was thus in many ways a travesty, and struck a broad spectrum of Zionists as such.

When, therefore, Buber, Feiwel and Weizmann arranged a letter of protest against Nordau's attack, published in *Ha-Zeman*, it was signed by a great number of the most prominent Zionists, not only on the cultural side. Yet it was the cultural wing which was most deeply antagonized by Nordau's attack, and the controversy over *Altneuland* meant that the book, instead of providing the rallying call which Herzl had intended, became a symbol of division, between the political Zionists, mostly Western and Central European supporters of Herzl, and the cultural Zionists, largely Eastern European supporters of Ahad Ha'am.[4]

This division had been there implicitly from the first. Zionism did, after all, pre-date Herzl by many years, and the Lovers of Zion had, as we have seen, a quite different approach to the Jewish problem. Herzl's sheer audacity in claiming the leadership, and his willpower in welding the disparate strands of Zionism into a coherent force had, until 1902 and the *Altneuland* controversy, put the continuing differences in approach in the shade. Until the Fifth Congress of 1901, what was striking about the movement was that it was there at all, and that it was as united in its aims as it was.

Nor should one forget what Herzl and his opponents had in common. On Herzl's side, he had become convinced that the only proper homeland for the Jews could be Palestine. To this end he supported the setting up of the Jewish National Fund at the Fifth Congress, the purpose of which was to purchase land in Palestine.[5] The loving descriptions of the (potential) Palestinian landscape in *Altneuland* are further evidence of just how wedded Herzl had become to this goal. On the other side, a figure such as Buber, himself a man of Central Europe, although in a quite different manner, shared to some extent

Herzl's vision of Jews mediating between East and West, and having a universalist role to perform.

Yet there were definite differences, and these made their first major public appearance at the Fifth Congress, when the new Democratic Faction, led by Buber, Feiwel and Weizmann, and consisting of the cultural Zionists, walked out of the Congress over the neglect of their cultural programme by Herzl. At that time the differences were patched up by an outwardly conciliatory Herzl, but from this point on he did what he could to immobilize this disobedient faction. He was even the secret patron of the Orthodox Zionist movement, as a counter to the cultural Zionists among East European Jewry.[6] The *Altneuland* controversy was just one stage, if an important one, in the alienation of this group from the Herzlian leadership. It prepared the ground for the catastrophe of the Uganda episode.

At base, despite his nationalism and his devotion to Palestine, Herzl remained a rationalist liberal whose main concern was the rescuing of world Jewry from moral and physical disaster. It was Jewish need, and not Jewish culture or identity, which drove the Herzlian Zionist machine. To those Zionists who came from the Hibbat Zion tradition, or were under the influence of Ahad Ha'am's cultural perspective, the driving force of their Zionism was its goal of reclaiming the Jewish land in Palestine, either as a spiritual centre for all Jews in the world, or as a version, secular or religious, of the Messianic return. Herzl thought Zionism was possible, and necessary, because of Jewish suffering. To most of the Russian Zionists, suffering was secondary to the prospect of regaining Eretz Israel, and creating a viable Jewish culture.[7]

Until 1902, this difference in approach was not critical, because both sides were united in their pursuit, by political means, of 'a Jewish homeland recognized by public law in Palestine', as laid down in the Basel Programme of 1897. Starting in 1902, however, his hopes dashed for any prospects of a charter from the Turks for a Jewish settlement in Palestine proper, Herzl began to pursue seriously another strategy, which smacked much more of his original plan for a state of the Jews—wherever possible.[8]

While he constantly sought to persuade the Turks to give him a charter in Palestine, there was also, lurking in the background, an alternative: a Jewish settlement in Cyprus. The Cyprus plan was suggested to Herzl as early as 1898 by Davis Trietsch, after Herzl's initial failure with the Turks. At first he did not take much notice of the idea, as he had high hopes for the main prize of Palestine. However, when the German protectorate proposal fell through, Herzl felt bound to put the Cyprus plan informally to the delegates to the Third Zionist Congress in 1899, as a way of providing immediate help to the persecuted Jewish masses in Eastern Europe. The suggestion was firmly rejected. Yet Herzl returned to the idea again in 1901, seeing the island as a preparatory base for the Palestinian settlement. He even, at one point, thought of conquest of 'Eretz Israel', but was quick to reject this 'all too colourful idea'.[9]

The hopes raised by Herzl's visit to Constantinople in the summer of 1901, and again in February 1902, put off serious consideration of any such plan of a settlement 'next door'. The renewed failure of the Turkish negotiations, and the worsening plight of East European Jewry, led to Herzl seriously considering the Trietsch plan once more, this time with the inclusion, as well as Cyprus, of the Sinai Peninsula and the Wadi el Arish (or Brook of Egypt) as areas of settlement. All were, in effect, parts of the British Empire, and so it was to the British government, the most liberal in Europe, and ruling the one society which was not, as yet, openly anti-Semitic, that Herzl turned in the summer of 1902.

It was a propitious moment. The English establishment, though loth to admit that they were anti-Semitic, were increasingly concerned about the immigration of 'poor foreigners' and its effect on the labour market. In other words, they felt threatened by the influx of East European Jews, fleeing from abject poverty and persecution to the most liberal and richest country in the world. A Royal Commission had been set up to look into the question of whether restrictions were necessary on immigration (unheard of in England up to that point), and Herzl had been invited (through the offices of English Zionists) to be an expert witness before the Commission. Through this device, Herzl managed finally to meet Nathaniel Meyer, Lord Rothschild, and at this meeting won Rothschild's support for his plan for Jewish colonies in the British territories neighbouring Palestine. As Herzl wrote in his diary afterwards: 'That was victory.'[10] After a brief and fruitless sojourn in Constantinople, Herzl was back in England in October, where he had an interview with Joseph Chamberlain, the Colonial Secretary. This was followed by an interview with Lord Lansdowne, the Foreign Secretary, and the upshot was 'the colossal fact' that the British government would seriously consider a Jewish settlement in El Arish, if Lord Cromer, the Consul General and effective ruler of Egypt, agreed.

There followed months of elation for Herzl, as he thought himself on the brink of setting up the Jewish settlement, if not in Palestine at least in Egyptian Palestine. The disappointment in May, when the El Arish plan fell apart on the difficulties of irrigation and the opposition of Lord Cromer, was thus even harder to take than previous failures, with the Germans in 1898 and the Turks in 1901. As Herzl wrote in May 1903: 'And I thought the Sinai project so certain that I would not buy any more space in the Döblinger cemetery, where my father is provisionally laid to rest. Now I consider the plan so definite a failure that I have been at the district court and have acquired vault 28.'[11]

The situation was made worse by the atrocities of the Kishinev pogrom in April 1903. Here was the barbarous, physical attack on Jews which Herzl had feared, and against which he had warned. The collapse of the El Arish project meant, however, that Zionism still had no remedy to the immense distress of its main constituency, the persecuted Jewish masses of the East. It was under these conditions that Herzl began seriously to consider the Uganda option. As he was later to write to Nordau: 'We must give an answer to Kishinev, and this is the only one ... We must, in a word, play the politics of the hour.'[12] The extent of the changed circumstances can be gauged by the fact that when Lord Rothschild originally suggested Uganda as an option in the summer of 1902, Herzl had rejected it out of hand. When, however, Chamberlain repeated the offer of a territory in East Africa (called at that time Uganda, but in present-day Kenya) in May 1903, Herzl took one of his gambles, a fateful one as it turned out, and agreed to negotiate.

Back in October 1902, at his original interview with Chamberlain, Herzl had told the Colonial Secretary: 'Now I have time to negociate [sic], but my people has not. They are starving in the Pale. I must bring them an immediate help.'[13] This was even more true in the summer of 1903. Indeed by now it was clear that Herzl, with an increasingly ominous heart complaint, could not wait either. Time was running out for him as well as his people. He had to do something for the Jews, or else die a failure, a terrible fate for a man who depended so much on success. It is against this background of personal and political desperation that Herzl's agreement to consider Uganda should be understood.

It must be stressed that at no time did Herzl see Uganda as an alternative to Palestine. Instead, if he ever seriously contemplated a Jewish colony in East Africa, and this is open to question, it would only have been an emergency staging post, where Jews could gather under the 'flag of Zion', and then wait to colonize the homeland. In a letter to Nordau he likened this 'strategic detour' to 'an inverted England in miniature', with the colonies being founded before the homeland. In that respect it is of note that Herzl also approached Portugal, Belgium and Italy for possible colonial charters in various areas of Africa.[14] Yet the actual realization of a Ugandan colony was not Herzl's prime aim.

He viewed it rather as a diversionary tactic of diplomacy, on the one hand to provide a bargaining counter with the Turks, on the other to make the British government, the most powerful and respected in the world at the time, and with great influence over Middle Eastern politics, an ally of Zionism. As he wrote to Nordau: 'If we acknowledge Chamberlain's offer with thanks, retaining the mentioned conditions, we strengthen our position in his sympathies, we involve him in the necessity of doing something for us in the event that *our* commission (which we have under our control) brings in a negative recommendation; and we have, in our relationship with this gigantic nation, acquired recognition as a state-building power (cf. in international law the quality of a war-waging power).'[15] It was indeed a phenomenal diplomatic coup for Herzl and his Zionist organization to gain official British government recognition as the representatives of the Jewish people. In his view the apparent retreat from Palestine was more than compensated for by this international recognition, which might have unforeseeable—positive—consequences.

At the same time, Herzl tried all he could to exert pressure on Turkey to give him a charter to settle Palestine. This was one of the main reasons for his trip to Russia, during which he met Plehve, the Interior Minister, obtaining from him a letter supporting the Zionist policy of emigration and promising help with the Turks. Yet this trip also confirmed, in Herzl's view, the pressing need of the Jewish masses for relief from poverty and persecution. He was deeply moved by the emotional reception which the Jews of Vilna gave him, but also by the overwhelming evidence of their desperate situation. It was with a conviction even stronger than before that something had to be done for the Jewish masses of the East, and armed with the British offer of Uganda and Plehve's letter, that he approached the fateful Sixth Congress in August 1903.

He set out his response to the emergency situation in his opening address to the Congress. Kishinev had shown how critical the Jewish position had become. So many Jews had fled that England and the United States had imposed restrictions on immigration despite themselves. Negotiations with

Turkey had failed. El Arish had failed. Now, there was the offer of land for an autonomous colony in East Africa. This had none of the 'historical, poetic-religious and Zionist value' of Palestine, which would still be the 'final goal'. Yet this was an emergency, needing emergency measures, and having the added benefit that Britain now recognized the movement. 'Admittedly this is not Zion, and it can never become so. It is only a colonization stop-gap, but, be it noted, on a national and state foundation.' Herzl further tried to reassure the Congress by stressing the help which could be expected from the Russians over Turkey's attitude to Palestine. Efforts directed towards Palestine should, therefore, be continued. For the time being, however, 'the statesmanlike generosity' of the British should be answered by the Congress agreeing to send a commission to Africa to review the possibility of a colony there.[16]

When the sending of an exploratory expedition was eventually voted on, Herzl won a large majority, 295 to 177. Yet he achieved this at the price of seeing the opposition, including most of the Russian contingent, walk out of the Congress. To these people, any diversion from Palestine was a betrayal of the whole movement, indeed made it meaningless. The goal of Zionism had to be the Jewish homeland in Palestine, as set down in the Basel Programme. No amount of Jewish suffering ought to divert Zionism from this purpose. What made the situation truly ironic was that those people who so decisively rejected Herzl's Uganda ploy were the representatives of the very East European Jews for whom this *Nachtasyl*,* as Nordau famously called it, had been intended. The Zionists from Kishinev were among those who opposed Herzl's emergency measure. The exit of the Russians thus not only threatened a disastrous split, but made the whole East African gambit, as a real emergency measure, pointless.[17]

Herzl managed to swallow his pride, and in an extra-

---

* Literally 'night shelter', but with the unfortunate sense of 'doss-house'.

ordinary effort of self-control and leadership persuaded the
rebels to return to the Congress. He cemented the reconciliation with one of his most famous dramatic gestures.
During his closing speech at the Congress he raised his right
hand and exclaimed: 'If I forget thee, O Jerusalem, may my
right hand forget itself.'[18] Yet it was clear that the restored
unity was only surface deep. The Uganda question went to
the heart of the division within Zionism, which would later
be the question over which the movement split. Was Zionism
a movement to rescue Jewish individuals from persecution
and insecurity, and set up their own state so that they could
become a normal, even a model people? Or was it a quasi-
religious return to the Holy Land, where the priority had to
be to regain contact with the soil of the Promised Land? The
opponents of the Uganda project clearly adhered to the latter
interpretation, and it was this group, mainly Russian, which
was to become the dominant force in Zionism from now on.
Herzl, on the other hand, despite the outward reconciliation
achieved, was in private distraught about the way in which
the stand-off at the Sixth Congress in effect meant the sacri-
ficing of the humanitarian option in favour of the Russians'
religio-cultural goal.

What was even worse was the fact that the split in the
movement went straight through him. Although still the
liberal rationalist of Der Judenstaat, Herzl had been deeply
affected by his experience of East European Jewry, not least in
his deeply moving meeting of them at first hand in Vilna,
where he even tells of a 'ghetto with good ghetto talks'—this
from a man who had run from the ghetto all his life, before
and after discovering Zionism.[19] Moreover he admired the
sheer idealism and willpower of his Russian opponents, their
sheer tenacity in the face of oppression.[20] Yet he could not see
why they could not accept that, in an emergency, there could
be an interim solution.

He told his closest friends after the Congress what he would
say at the next, Seventh Congress. 'By that time I shall have
Palestine, or else I shall have recognized the complete futility

of all further effort in that direction. In this latter case the summary of my speech will be: It was not possible. The ultimate goal has not been reached and cannot be reached within the foreseeable future. But we have a compromise achievement—this land in which our suffering masses can be settled on a national foundation with autonomous rights. I do not believe that for the sake of a beautiful dream or a legitimist flag we ought to withhold relief from the unfortunate. But I understand at the same time that this has brought a decisive split into our movement, and this division passes straight through my person. Although I was originally a Jewish statist, *n'import où*, I did later on lift up the flag of Zion, and I myself became a Lover of Zion. Palestine is the one land where our people can come to rest. But hundreds of thousands are waiting for immediate help.'[21] The only solution he could envisage was that he resign and that the movement, in effect, split in two. This is more or less what was to happen.

In the months that followed the Sixth Congress, the crisis refused to go away: indeed, it sharpened. The smouldering resentment and suspicion of Herzl's opponents were made public in an open letter from Menachem Ussishkin, one of the most prominent Russian Zionists, and Herzl's model for Mendel, the honest but stupid peasant in *Altneuland*. Ussishkin, who was for a policy of settlement first and official recognition second, the pre-Herzlian Hibbat Zion strategy, announced that he would not regard as binding the Uganda resolution of the Congress, for the sending of 'an expedition to any other country is a renunciation of Palestine and a separation from it'. It was Palestine or nothing.

Herzl replied in a stinging attack, published with Ussishkin's letter in *Die Welt* in October 1903. He vigorously defended his diplomatic approach to the search for a Jewish homeland, saying that in politics one had to act politically (which shows just how much he remained a liberal). At the same time, he vehemently attacked Ussishkin's activities in Palestine, stating that having too high a profile there, whether it be in the form of a Palestinian Congress or land purchase, would only damage the Zionist cause, without the acquisition of a charter. Land purchase was acceptable, and indeed Herzl supported it, but only if it was low-key. It could never achieve the main aim, which must be sovereignty. Private and national acquisition of land were two qualitatively different things. What Herzl was saying was something which many have not grasped to this day: no matter how much land the Jews were to own in Palestine, as long as they did not have a charter, a legal right to rule there, it would not be the Jewish homeland envisaged in the Basel Programme. It was precisely this perception of the difference between private and national land acquisition 'which constitutes the crux of our movement', as Herzl rightly pointed out.[22]

Herzl's reply went to the heart of his view of Zionism as a respectable, legal movement, intent on achieving its aims with, and not against, international society. Yet the general reaction was not very favourable, and one can see why. Herzl was dealing from a very weak hand. He had tried, allusively, to justify the Uganda project as a way of getting the Turks to be more reasonable about granting a charter, as a ploy in property negotiations, yet this only raised more questions, and failed to answer Ussishkin's main point: that it had to be Palestine or nothing. Herzl had painted himself into a corner. If Uganda was indeed to become a Jewish colony, then its realization would require an immense effort, and it was foreseeable that Palestine would fade into the background for some time, perhaps for ever. If, on the other hand, Uganda was merely a ploy, not seriously meant, then Herzl was endangering the movement's unity, and good relations with the British, for nothing of substance. This was the kind of game diplomats could play, but not the leaders of purportedly democratic movements such as Zionism had become.

Herzl knew this only too well, after the event. He knew, for instance, that the Russian Jews were not with him for Uganda, but only for Palestine. As he told Kireyev: 'They will not budge for a rich empire in Africa, but they will go on their knees to the arid land of our ancestors. In sum,' he added with respect, 'this trait of character is not one of the lowest.'[23] His response to the furore over his bout with Ussishkin was to write a 'Letter to the Jewish people' to explain his position. This was to be a public version of what he had told his circle of close friends after the Congress, with some points added. He claimed, rather questionably, that in 1901 he could have obtained a charter for Palestine from the Turks, if only the Jews had given him the money required. They had not. 'Because you did not will it, it remains a legend, for this period.' Yet Zionism existed, and the movement ought to do something for the Jewish masses in their distress. 'But this can be done only if there is firm ground—land—under our feet.' Hence the need for a territory, even in Uganda. Herzl, on the other hand, who remained intent on Palestine despite every-thing, could not lead the movement to Uganda if those who were the strongest proponents of Palestine split from the movement. If there was, therefore, a split, he would have to resign. If this happened 'my heart remains with the Zionists and my reason with the Africans.'[24]

This touching, tragic document was never made public, because the revolt of the Russian Zionists, at the Charkov conference, intervened. The resolutions of this rebel confer-ence constituted a comprehensive attack on Herzl's leadership and his policy. They demanded more democratic control of the movement, and an exclusive concentration on Palestine as the only acceptable territorial goal. Meanwhile, just as the Russians were putting Herzl in a position where it was impossible to back down, it was becoming more and more obvious that the British were having second, and third, thoughts about their Uganda offer. The white settlers already in Kenya were aghast at the prospect of a Jewish colony, on good land, and their protest had led to a noticeable cooling of British interest in granting an East African charter. Herzl's response was one of relief, for now he could get his emissary, Leopold Greenberg, to press again for Sinai, and also redouble his own efforts with the Turks, which he had never given up completely. The attempted assassination of Nordau in

December shifted the sympathy of the movement to Herzl's side again, but left him even more unable to signal the failure of the Uganda proposal, in case this looked like capitulation to the Charkovites. In private, Herzl was doing his best to end the Uganda project; in public he was in open warfare with the Russian rebels. His reception of the Charkov delegation on New Year's Eve 1903 was cordial but unbending: 'I kicked them out with superb politeness.'[25]

Herzl in January and February of 1904 gives the impression of a gambler whose luck has run out, a sorcerer's apprentice too worn out to stem any longer the flood of events. On the one hand there was open rebellion in Russia, on the other Herzl was now trying to ensure that the Uganda project failed, when Greenberg and the British were doing their best to salvage at least something from it. It was thus very bad news when a British offer was actually made, and perforce accepted, in early February 1904, for everyone around Herzl, and Herzl himself, knew that the project was in any case doomed to failure. By just going through the motions, however, Zionism was being torn apart. At the end of February Herzl made one last effort to save the day, by calling a meeting of the Greater Actions Committee, which met on 11 April.

Herzl's handling of this meeting was his last great performance as a Zionist leader. His opening statement was an offer of peace. He justified the Uganda project yet again as an emergency measure, while fervently professing his adherence to Palestine as the final goal. Above all, he pleaded, the movement required unity, and this meant that the opposition must adhere to the decisions of the Congress. In his closing statement, on 12 April, he again stressed the need for unity, and now he stressed what he had given to Zionism. Before him, the Zionists had been a loose amalgam of idealistic and ineffectual groups. He had shown them the 'path to the objective. This path is the organization of the people, and its organ is the Congress.' He would not, he continued, go to Uganda, but even if he did so, he could never be accused of being

unfaithful to Palestine: 'It was as a *Judenstaatler*★ that I presented myself to you. I gave you my card, and there the words
were printed: "Herzl, *Judenstaatler*". In the course of time I
learned a great deal. First and foremost I learned to know
Jews, and that was sometimes even a pleasure. But above all, I
learned to understand that we shall find the solution of our
problem only in Palestine.' They should believe him, and trust
him, and come back into the fold. The meeting ended with
Herzl promising a free discussion of the Uganda project at the
Seventh Congress, and the Russians accepting his leadership
again. Reconciliation had been achieved.[26]

A few weeks later his medical condition took a turn for the
worse. Herzl eventually died on 3 July, 1904.

His death, at the age of 44, caused profound shock and grief
in the world Jewish community, especially in Eastern Europe.
On the day of his funeral Vienna was swamped with Jews
from all over the world who had come to mourn their leader.
Among those present, apart from most of the Zionist leadership, including Martin Buber and Stephen Wise, were
Hermann Bahr, the antagonist of Herzl's youth, but later his
friend; Arthur Schnitzler, his erstwhile confidant; and Moritz
Benedikt, the editor of the *Neue Freie Presse*, with most of
the staff of the newspaper Herzl had worked for during all
his Zionist years.

It is usually said of the *Neue Freie Presse* that the only
mention of Herzl's Zionism it ever printed was a mean couple
of lines in their obituary of him. This is not so. A feuilleton
was printed on the day of his funeral, written by a colleague,
which stated categorically that it would be 'almost foolish' to
talk of Herzl and not mention Zionism. The interpretation of
Herzl's Zionist impulse given in this eulogy is a fascinating
one. It was due to his pride, remarks the author, that Herzl
came to feel sympathy, and to identify, with his persecuted
fellow Jews. 'Messianic urgings' led to his confronting himself
with the mission to 'lead his people from the desert of misery

★ Roughly: a supporter of the idea of a state of the Jews, anywhere.

back to the Promised Land'. 'The rights of a thousand years, acquired in unspeakable suffering, were to be thrown away for the pursuit of a beautiful dream from the far Orient. Pride would have been better served, if not more nobly, by a staunch defence of these rights. But our friend preferred the more refined attitude, the more handsome posture, as befitted his artistic nature. For he remained an artist, even in his quest for this shadow. He believed he could rebuild the state of the Jews as if it were an architectonic work of art. It was astounding with what tenacity he held to his dream.' Written three days after Herzl's death, this is a remarkable portrayal of Herzl the Zionist, and presages most of the literature on Herzl the 'artist-politician'. The eulogy ends with the words 'he was too proud, much too proud, not to be a good human being (*Mensch*).'[27]

Also present at the funeral was Stefan Zweig, who was deeply moved by the immense outpouring of grief among the Jewish crowd there, and was later to give voice in his memoirs to another aspect of Herzl: 'This immense pain rising out of the depths of an entire people made me realize for the first time how much passion and hope this singular and lonely man had given to the world by the power of his idea.'[28]

Herzl left a troubled legacy to both his family and his movement. His wife and children were left destitute on his death, for Herzl had sunk all he had into Zionism. The movement had to launch an appeal on their behalf. Julie, Herzl's wife, only outlived her husband by three years, dying at the age of 39 in 1907. In accordance with her will she was cremated; her son Hans left the urn containing her remains on a train. The eldest child, Pauline, ended up a morphine addict in Bordeaux, where she died in 1930. Hans underwent circumcision at the age of fifteen, was educated in England, gaining a degree at Cambridge, was psychoanalysed by Freud, and in 1924 converted to the Baptist sect of Christianity, the first of a series of conversions which ultimately led him back to the Liberal Jewish Synagogue in London. He committed suicide in 1930, on the day of his sister Pauline's funeral. The fate of Trude, the youngest child, was perhaps the most tragic of all: after marrying a Jewish industrialist and giving birth to a son, Stephen Theodor Neumann, she spent the rest of her life in Vienna's psychiatric hospital, Am Steinhof, until she was deported by the Nazis in 1942 to the concentration camp, or 'ghetto', of Terezin (Theresienstadt), where she died in early 1943. Her son, Herzl's grandson, also educated at Cambridge, committed suicide in Washington DC in 1946. Thus ended the Herzl succession.[29]

It is hard to know how much of this family tragedy can be blamed on Herzl, and it might also be said that what his family did after his death should have no effect on how we view him as a 'Jewish thinker'. The consequences of his legacy to his movement are a different matter. The initial results were not good. Without its leader, the unity of the movement soon collapsed. At the Seventh Congress in 1905 the 'Territorialists', the supporters of the Uganda option led by Israel Zangwill, seceded. Yet if the movement thus fractured, it did not completely fall apart. Instead, in no small way due to the permanent institutions which Herzl's organizational efforts had done so much to bring about, the movement survived. Admittedly it was, in its post-Herzlian form, greatly changed, with Herzl's version no longer being the dominant one. Zionism was now exclusively intent on Palestine, with the main division being between the 'political' Zionists, who saw themselves as the successors to Herzl's diplomatic strategy, and the 'practical' Zionists, who were for a gradual colonization of Palestine, regardless of the diplomatic situation. At the Seventh Congress a compromise between these two factions was reached, albeit an uneasy one.

'Practical' Zionism, a return to the original Hibbat Zion strategy, was the ascendant wing from then until the Tenth Zionist Congress in 1911. With the resignation of Herzl's successor, David Wolffsohn, and Herzl's former lieutenant, Max Nordau, at that congress, 'practical' Zionism's ascendancy turned into dominance, with Herzl's strictures against 'infiltration' largely ignored by the now overwhelmingly Eastern European leadership. Even so, Herzl's vision was not completely forgotten. The legacy of his political strategy remained as policy, although it lapsed into abeyance. Negotiations with the Turks continued, and links to the governments of Europe were kept up, especially with the British. The contacts which had been made in 1902 by Greenberg and Herzl eventually led, by way of Chaim Weizmann, to the Balfour Declaration of 1917, of which Herzl can thus lay some claim to being the posthumous architect.[30] In 1948 the state of the Jews, Israel, was formally declared, and, crucially from a Herzlian perspective, recognized by the United Nations. Herzl, as the founder of the Zionist movement, became the father of the new state of Israel. Although with many ironies and complications, his spirit informs it still.

7

CONCLUSION

In the midst of the Uganda crisis, in January 1904, Herzl travelled to Italy. He finally had the audience with the Pope which had been an ambition of his long before he became a Zionist. Back in 1893 he had envisaged asking the Pope to collaborate in the mass conversion of the Jews to Christianity. Now, a decade later, he sought the Pope's help in obtaining a Jewish homeland. The audience was not a particular success. Herzl refused to kiss the Pope's hand, and the Pope declined to favour the Zionist project, despite Herzl's assurances about the extra-territoriality of the Holy Places. Herzl, however, had two further audiences in Rome, which both say something interesting about his character.

In the first of these, with Cardinal Merry del Val, Herzl responded to del Val's propounding of the official position of the Church, that the Jews could not be helped by the Church unless they converted, by using a remarkable argument. He likened the Jews' adherence to their faith to the man who refuses to give up his coat in a gale, but who will take it off when the sun shines on him. Persecution, he told the Papal Secretary, had not made Jews convert, but perhaps a benevolent attitude to them, and, by implication, to Zionism, might. 'Were the Church to behave towards the Jews with generosity and kindness—the conquest might be successful precisely among the more noble natures.'[1] Of course, this was Herzl being the diplomat, trying any argument he could to gain papal support, yet it is a phenomenal thing for the leader of Zionism to do: to hold out the prospect of Jewish conversion as an incentive for good treatment of the Jews by the

Catholic Church. At the same time, it is an almost eerie echo of Herzl's original, assimilatory motive for seeking the backing of the Pope. There was a great deal of continuity between the pre-Zionist Herzl and the Zionist leader, more, perhaps, than he was aware of, or willing to admit.

The other major audience which Herzl had in Rome was with King Victor Emmanuel III. It is clear from his diary account that Herzl greatly enjoyed meeting this affable, straightforward and quick-witted man. They discussed how to deal with the Turks, and the King revealed a certain scepticism about Herzl's insistence on being above board. They also, after a disquisition by Herzl on *Altneuland*, discussed the figure of Shabbetai Zvi. Victor Emmanuel revealed that one of his ancestors had been a co-conspirator of Shabbetai. 'He wanted to become King of Macedonia, Cyprus, I don't know, some sort of king anyway. He was a little crazy,' he added, 'but he thought big.' No doubt with a twinkle in his eye, he then asked Herzl whether the Jews still expected a Messiah. Herzl replied that in religious circles this was the case, 'but in ours, that of the educated and enlightened, there is, of course, none of this.' On realizing that Victor Emmanuel had thought him some kind of rabbi, Herzl was quick to correct him: 'No, no, sire, the movement is purely national.' Herzl now felt that he had to make it quite clear to the king that Zionism was not a kind of false Messianism, as the king, it seems, had suspected. 'And to his amusement, I told him how, while in Palestine, I had avoided mounting a white donkey or white horse, so that I was not burdened with being thought the Messiah. He laughed.'[2]

Herzl's views in this audience can, of course, as with the del Val audience, be dismissed as mere politicking. We have seen how, on other occasions, Herzl was prepared to emphasize much more the religious aspects of Zionism, including the Messianic idea. In the presence of the head of a secular, indeed anti-clerical state, on the other hand, Herzl was no doubt wise to play down any such religious side. Yet his description of his attempts to discourage the idea that he was the Messiah rings true. There is, in the recognition of the significance of the white donkey or horse, the Herzlian sensitivity to the importance of appearances; and there is also the Herzlian realization that he might indeed be taken by his followers to be the Messiah. There is even a sense of the lurking temptation to see himself as such.[3] At the same time, however, there is the effort to resist such dreams, and the recognition of the necessity to keep the movement away, as much as possible, from the business of religious prophecy. It is but one more example of Herzl's constant struggle to keep rational control over the powerful and irrational mass-political forces which his leadership of Zionism stirred up.

Herzl's was a life full of tensions. In Budapest he grew up as an assimilated Jew between German and Hungarian. In Vienna, his attempt to participate fully in the life and culture of his colleagues, by being a German nationalist, foundered on his Jewishness. He did not become the ultimate Viennese; instead he became the ultimate Viennese Jewish journalist. His attempt to gain recognition as a German writer, and thus acceptance in society as a whole, was compromised by the fact that this strategy, the seeking of fame, itself became a Jewish phenomenon in Vienna.[4] Even during his years in Paris, when his Jewishness on a personal level went 'unrecognized', he lived with the fact that his journalism created the ambition in him to be a politician, yet his Jewishness made any such plans seem impossible in his Austrian homeland.

Zionism provided a solution to these personal, accumulated conflicts, as much as to the Jewish problem generally. It allowed Herzl to be a politician. It also meant that he could be a German writer, albeit on Zionist themes, as in *Altneuland*, and envisage being a German still, 'over there'. As leader of Zionism, and hence of the Jewish people, in his own mind, Herzl could also satisfy his own need for recognition and social acceptance by achieving for his Jewish people recognition and acceptance by international society. That there was a link between the personal and the national desire for recognition is spelled out clearly in the *Futuro* episode in *Altneuland*, where Jo Levy, although he orchestrates the whole settlement, and organizes the *Futuro* expedition, never, in a narrative filled with pathos, actually meets the world's cultural élite, and is even unsure that he has seen the ship.[5] This is Herzl's metaphor of his fears that he will, as Moses before him, never personally experience the achievement of his goal, but the goal is not so much establishing a Jewish homeland—Levy does this—as coming face to face with world approval, world recognition.

The identification with Moses, self-willed, also tells us something about what Zionism did not resolve for Herzl. The 'Parnell of the Jews' always remained at a distance from the people he led. If he was not an Egyptian prince, he nevertheless, as an assimilated Viennese journalist, came with attitudes to his Jewishness quite different from those of his East European followers. If he at least partially solved some of his personal tensions by embracing Zionism, his discovery of what the Jewish people, and Zionism, were in actuality, revealed the historical tension between Western and Central European Jewry on the one hand, and Eastern European Jewry on the other, which was to dominate the Zionist movement under his leadership. This was a dynamic and powerful tension, which did much to drive the movement forward, and which Herzl was initially able to direct. Ultimately, however, the movement broke in his hands in the Uganda crisis, precisely over this division.

Herzl was not devoid of religious motivation. He too, as has been the central contention of this book, was intent on realizing the 'Jewish mission' of the modern Central European Jewish tradition. Yet this was not religious motivation in the traditional sense, but rather in an abstract, 'world-historical' one. His view of history was as teleological as that of the traditionalists, but his God remained to the end the 'will to good', and his view of the historical necessity and inevitability of the state of the Jews remained centred on the benefits of this to humanity. Although Herzl was, as we have also seen, not unaffected by his experience of traditional Jewish ideas, considerations of these remained secondary, even peripheral. It is quite true that Herzl became convinced that Palestine had to be the Jewish homeland. Religious traditions clearly played a large part here, not only because of Herzl's recognition that this was the only goal acceptable to Jews, but also because of his own emotional attachment to that end. Yet his 'love of Zion' was based on general historical and cultural considerations, not on tradition as such. Palestine was not the goal because certain areas prescribed in the Bible had been the land of Judea: there is no sense in his writings that he ever worried about the exact borders of the new Jewish homeland. It simply made sense of history for the Jews to set up a model state of freedom in the area of the world which had been their old home.

He certainly saw himself fulfilling a religiously sanctioned role, and there was something messianic about his perception of this. The rebuilding of the Temple in *Altneuland*, 'because the fullness of time had come', and his intimation in the same book that the people of Israel were their own Messiah, are indications of a messianic dimension.[6] Yet Herzl's messianism was essentially a historical, modern type, akin to the kind of secular messianism which affected contemporary socialism. He saw himself not so much as the Messiah, but rather as a man of history, making modern sense of old religious super-stition, giving the Messianic myth its proper, historical meaning and realization.[7]

With his abstract understanding of religion, Herzl could never fully come to terms with the immense religious power behind the idea of the return to Zion. Whether this is because he underestimated the power of tradition, or could not ade-quately control it, is open to question. His espousal, his very contemplation of the Uganda option, suggests the former, his careful avoidance of being seen as the Messiah the latter. Whichever is the case, the fact remains that the Messianic overtones which Herzl tried to control, and the rejection of any other goal than Palestine which threatened his leadership in the Uganda crisis, were both the result of the strong influence which traditional religion had on Eastern European Zionists, even when they claimed to be completely liberated from religious belief.[8] Herzl died with the struggle in the movement between his essentially Central European, emancipatory view and that of his mainly Eastern European opponents unresolved. It remains unresolved in Israel to this day, and among Jews everywhere.

Herzl was a thinker who loved to look forward. Looking back on his thought from the perspective of the current times, one is struck by the huge ambivalences and ironies of Herzl's relationship to posterity. His interpretation of the Jewish question as the inevitable failure of assimilationism, with the only solution being the national solution, can in one sense be seen as prescient. We are, after all, living in a post-Holocaust age, in which there is a Jewish state. The identification with this Jewish state of Israel has, as Herzl predicted, served to strengthen Jewish identity throughout the world, and much of the rationale for that state has been to avoid Jews ever again being caught in the condition of helplessness in which they were between 1939 and 1945. It is doubtful, however, that Herzl ever seriously contemplated the possibility that anti-Semitism would lead to the attempt at the complete extermination of the Jewish people. Indeed he expressly rejects this. As Arthur Hertzberg has pointed out, the very historical inevitability of the state of the Jews in Herzl's scheme depends on the fact that the European states will be unable to attack the Jews physically. There will be mass distress, and informal persecution, as well as pogroms, but civilization is nevertheless too far advanced, and the Jews too much of a threat, financially and as potential socialist revolutionaries, for European states to sponsor officially the repeal of emancipation, let alone mass extermination. This is why they will accede to the externalizing of the Jewish problem in the form of an internationally recognized state of the Jews. Herzl was too much a man of his relatively civilized times to have predicted that the Germans, of all people, would perpetrate genocide on the Jews.[9]

If Herzl was over-optimistic about the consequences of the anti-Semitic forces which he so perceptively identified, he was also, strange as it may seem, too pessimistic about the viability of Jewish assimilation into Western societies. In order to disarm his assimilationist critics, he was prepared to allow that some Jews could assimilate successfully into Western society. But then they would not be Jewish. For the bulk of Jews, assimilation was impossible, he claimed, and in any case it was never desirable. Consequently, Herzl was convinced that only in their own state could Jews be Jews. For Jews to live as Jews in a non-Jewish society, even if it was England or America, claimed Herzl, would inevitably lead to anti-Semitism, and the kind of moral and physical plight which had been the experience of Jews throughout Europe. His experience of Vienna had shown him that even when Jews were 'assimilated', they remained hopelessly divorced from the society around them, and exerted an unhealthy influence on that society. Jews had either to assimilate completely, convert and 'submerge themselves', or leave to form their own society. Nothing in between would do.

It is difficult, from the viewpoint of democratic pluralism as now practised in most Western democracies, and especially in the United States, to agree with Herzl here. Isaiah Berlin put the counter-argument very succinctly when, in answering the same argument as presented by Arthur Koestler, he pointed out that to see the Jewish question as a choice between such mutually exclusive alternatives was a complete denial of liberal pluralism. It was a Jewish individual's right, in a pluralist democracy, to espouse beliefs and an identity different from his fellow citizens. This was, indeed, the very essence of liberty. So to say, as Koestler had said, that the only logical options were conversion or emigration to Israel, was a denial of liberal democracy.[10] This is not to say that Herzl did not have a point when he doubted that Jews could ever completely assimilate. It is, however, a denial of the conclusion which he drew from this, that emancipation is impossible within a Western, non-Jewish state. But then Herzl badly misjudged the potential of the Western liberal states, the United States especially, to live up to their liberal, and these days pluralist, precepts.

Herzl might have had a point when he said that only with the national emancipation embodied in a state of the Jews will the Jewish problem be fully solved, the Jewish individual completely 'inwardly free' from the tensions of being a Jew in the Diaspora. Yet, as his erstwhile confidant Arthur Schnitzler might have said, those tensions were precisely what made the Jews the 'ferment of humanity', the great contributors to modern thought and culture, which they were, and continue to be in the twentieth century. If Jews in the United States and other Western countries today still have inner tensions about their Jewishness, perhaps this is not as bad a thing as Herzl thought: Perhaps, indeed, it is a good thing. Without it much of the creativity and profundity of modern culture would be missing.

Conversely, when one looks at the Jewish state Herzl did so much to help bring about, one is struck by how much, especially in recent years, the reality has come short of his ideal vision. When Alex Bein wrote his biography of Herzl between the wars much of Herzl's liberal, secular and socially just vision seemed to be a fairly accurate, self-fulfilling prophecy. In 1962 Joseph Adler could see the opportunity for Israel to realize Herzl's dream, but also the threat that it might not.[11] Today it is sometimes painful to compare the hopes and the reality. Herzl wanted the army and religion to be kept out of politics. He envisaged the Holy Places being given an extra-territorial status. Above all he wanted the state of the Jews to be a paragon of tolerance to all. The incursion of religion into Israeli politics and the central place of the army in national life are a travesty of Herzl's intentions. Recent events in Jerusalem have exacerbated the troubled status of that city, which Herzl's idea of extra-territoriality might have solved. The final paradox, however, concerns Herzl's supreme ideal, of the state of the Jews as a means to, and a model of, tolerance.

Herzl's whole theory was based on the assumption that a

state of the Jews was necessary because otherwise Jews could never escape anti-Semitism. As he thought the American example showed, Jews trying to escape anti-Semitism simply brought it with them. When England finally succumbed to the inevitable, there would be nowhere in the world where Jews were not persecuted. Zionism solved the problem of anti-Semitism by removing its cause: the Jews. Once gathered in their own Jewish homeland Jews could then, as a normal nation, interact with other nations, on a national level where they would be respected and look after themselves, stand on their own two feet as any other nation did. With reciprocity, the backing of their own state, Jews would be respected throughout the world, as citizens of another state. There would be no antagonism, because the abnormal position of the Jews would no longer exist, and there would no longer be the economic and social competition within other states which had so exacerbated hatred against Jews. The inner dialectic of emancipation and anti-Semitism would thus find an external synthesis, by, in effect, a Jewish colonial policy. The Zionist bank was, it might be noted, called the Jewish Colonial Trust.

There was also a colonial air about the other part to Herzl's equation, the idea that, on the *tabula rasa* of the new land, Jews could create a new society and new people. Herzl once wrote in his diary: 'The leading principle of my life: Whoever wants to change people, must change the conditions of their lives.'[12] Whereas in the 'new ghetto' of Jewish existence in Europe people were ruled by their 'circumstances', the beauty of Zionism for Herzl was that it would allow a society to be built from scratch, with new conditions quite independent of the past. As a result the individuals who populated this society would be free of all society's past problems, because they would be shaped by their environment. A new world meant a new people. It also meant a world of tolerance, justice and freedom.

If this was indeed Herzl's idea, then it was, once he accepted the goal of Palestine, deeply flawed from the beginning, because it ignored the fact that there was not and never could be a *tabula rasa*: the past was as present in Palestine as it was in Europe, if not more so. Zionism, in other words, as with all colonialisms, never really took account of the problem of what to do with the natives: the Palestinian Arabs. Herzl was once directly confronted with this by a Palestinian Arab, Yussef Ziah el-Khaldi, who in March 1899 wrote to Zadoc Khan, Chief Rabbi of France, that Zionism was a charming dream, but ignored the reality that Palestine was under Ottoman rule and was already inhabited. Moreover, Jerusalem had a religious significance for Muslims as well, and this meant that they would never willingly give it up. Herzl's reply was the same as he later gave in *Altneuland*, that the Jews would bring such prosperity to the area that this would make the Arabs prosperous as well, that there was room for all. The Arabs would soon come to see the benefits of Jewish settlement, and welcome it.[13] This argument was flawed on many grounds. For a start, it took no account of the religious significance for Muslims of Palestine, and of the need for Muslim rule in Palestine. Herzl never fully grasped the strength of this, as he never realized the full extent of the hold of religious ideals over his own followers when it came to the Holy Land. If he had, he would have had to admit that the force of circumstances was as difficult to counter here as it was in Europe, perhaps more so.

Not realizing the full depth of religious feeling of Muslims concerning Palestine was something for which a Western liberal such as Herzl might be partially excused. Yet there was another blind spot which is less easy to pardon. By his own argument concerning the nature of anti-Semitism, he should have foreseen that the Arabs would resist Jewish settlement, because, according to him, Jews brought anti-Semitism with them wherever they went. If Jews experienced anti-Semitism in the vast expanses of America, why should the small land of Palestine be any different?

One can argue that Herzl, like many other colonial thinkers of the time, regarded the native population as irrelevant, a nonentity. One can also argue, as has Walter Laqueur, that there were only (!) half a million Arabs living in Palestine at the time, and no sense of Palestinian Arab nationalism.[14] The millions of Jews which Herzl envisaged flocking to the Jewish homeland would have swamped this population, making their voice negligible. One can imagine that this was Herzl's actual assumption concerning the Arab population: they would become an insignificant number, surrounded by Jewish masses.[15] One can further say that he allowed himself to be deluded by Zionist reports about the favourable attitude of the Arabs to the Jews, and that he thought a state where Jews would be in the majority would be a different proposition to one where they were in the minority: their just and tolerant rule would provide no reason for protest from the minority.

None of this, however, can mask the naïveté, and even worse the self-contradictory nature, of Herzl's official, public answer to the Arab question. If no amount of prosperity could rescue the Jews from anti-Semitism in Europe, why expect it to solve the problem in Palestine? Even if there had been no religious obstacles on the part of Islam, this perception, which was inherent in Herzl's own thought, should have been cause enough for Herzl to rethink his ideas. As it stands, his New Society, where Jews and native Arabs live together in peace, is the Utopian mirage he always wanted to avoid, and it is so for the very reasons he himself had given for setting up the Zionist movement in the first place. If the emancipation had been at fault by not recognizing the need to alter radically the conditions, the circumstances, of Jewish life among Gentiles, then Herzl's Zionism was equally neglectful of the actual conditions, an Arab populace under a Muslim ruler, which obtained in Palestine. It was not a *tabula rasa*; and Herzl was wilfully naïve in thinking it ever could be.

Despite so much that is attractive in his thought—and there is, as I hope I have shown, a great deal—Herzl reveals himself on this issue, which has become central to the debate on Zionism, as an unrealistic thinker, or one who was more wishful, even wilful, than honest in his thought. The state which he did so much to help found reflects the same inconsistencies. Dedicated to liberal democracy and tolerance in its legal and political system, it finds itself forced into a policy of discrimination and military occupation. Even the argument over the West Bank and Gaza is in many ways the same debate as over Uganda—between the need for territory and the sanctity of the Promised Land. Only now it is much more serious.

Perhaps most poignantly, Zionism, supposedly the solution to the Jewish problem, has only succeeded in putting that problem on another level. The creation of the Jewish state has, as Herzl predicted, given modern Jewish identity a great boost, and done much to restore the sense of pride in being Jewish which Herzl so painfully felt was lacking. Yet is the new Zionist Jewish identity enough, and is it really Jewish? American critics, such as Jacob Neusner and Arthur Hertzberg, have recently echoed the old critique of Ahad Ha'am, and pointed out that identification with the secular state of Israel is not enough for a living, vibrant Jewish identity. Neusner has gone so far as to say that such a positive Jewish identity can be found just as well, perhaps more strongly, in the American Diaspora.[16] What appear intolerant, illiberal, and thus 'un-Jewish', policies on the part of the Israeli government have begun to alienate a large section of American Jewry, by far the most populous and wealthiest in the world, from its former stance of intimate identification with, and strong support for, the state of Israel. The Zionist identity of Jews, largely inspired by Herzl, is beginning to fray at the edges.

The most profound problem that Zionism has not solved, but only transferred, is that of Jewish security. Herzl once called the state of the Jews a 'world ghetto'.[17] It was not an image he often used, and for good reason. A 'world ghetto' suggests a community which is walled in, cut off from and surrounded by a hostile world. His ideal, in contrast, was a state of the Jews which would be open to the world, indeed at its centre, and at peace with all the nations. The state of the Jews was the solution because it satisfied everyone. Jews, in their own state, could provide for their own security, whereas before they had been exposed to the anti-Semitic masses. Yet the security provided would in any case be minimal, because once separated from the other nations the Jews would cease to be seen as a threat, and would become valued allies. That Israel has indeed become a kind of 'world ghetto', embattled and suspicious of the outside world, is a tragic commentary on Herzl's thought. What is even worse is that Israel has become so dependent on America, and on the moral and financial support of American Jewry—which should, after all, not even exist if Herzl had seen his dreams come true. That the Jewish state is at all dependent on the Diaspora for its security and its economic well-being is perhaps the greatest indictment of Herzl's thought.

In a way, though, one can hardly blame Herzl for present-day Israel; in one crucial respect, the need for legality and international guarantees, Zionism after Herzl largely departed from his policies. He, indeed, has provided one of the most acute critiques of what eventually transpired. Herzl was adamant that one condition must obtain before settlement started: the agreement of international society, and especially of the former sovereign of the territory, perforce the Ottoman Empire. Without this, Herzl predicted, there would never be the conditions which would allow the kind of liberal and tolerant society, living at peace with its neighbours, which he envisaged. He has been proved right. It can well be argued that, if Herzl's policy had been followed, the Zionists would never have been able to obtain the necessary conditions. Turkish agreement was always a pipe-dream; the eventual British agreement always ambivalent. It is also true that even a charter would not have solved the Arab problem, as became evident under the British mandate. Herzl's state of the Jews was always, perhaps, a dream. What is certain, however, is that Herzl was only too farsighted about the need for such international agreement, if the state of the Jews was to be the complete solution to the Jewish problem of which he dreamed; and if it was to be allowed to develop in peace and prosperity.

At times Zionism seemed close to this international agreement, as at the time of the Balfour Declaration, and then of the United Nations plan for partition. At other times, however, Herzl's heirs, ignoring his lessons about the need for international and legal recognition as a prerequisite, were only too willing to let the facts speak, and not worry about the legal and political conditions in which they acted. One should be aware of over-simplification in judging the complex history of the emergence of the state of Israel, and it is quite true that much effort was expended on gaining international recognition for the Jewish state, successfully, as the Israeli presence at the United Nations shows. In the end, however, one comes back to the fact that the Jewish state was not founded in conditions of prior international agreement, but rather in civil and international strife. Israelis, and Jews the world over, are still living with the consequences.

Perhaps this was inevitable, if the Jewish state was ever to be founded. Perhaps, as well, it is time to be reminded by the father of Israel about the importance of international opinion and good relations with its neighbours to the well-being of the Jewish state, the state of the Jews. There is still time, and there might yet, with goodwill on the part of Israel as well as its opponents, be peace. This will not be easy, but then was it not Herzl who said: 'If you wish it, it is no fairytale'? Perhaps only then, with the international agreement Herzl required, will the conditions be right for Herzl's dream to be truly realized, of a Jewish nation at peace with the world, and at peace with itself.

NOTES

Full bibliographical information will be found in the Select Bibliography, pp. 156–7.

1: *Living in the New Ghetto*

1 For the most detailed and recent description of Herzl's early years, see Andrew Handler, *Dori: the life and times of Theodor Herzl in Budapest (1860–1878)*, University of Alabama, 1983. See also Joseph Patai, 'Herzl's school years', in *Herzl Yearbook*, vol. 3, New York, 1960, pp. 53–75.

2 For a detailed and convincing exposition of the ideology of emancipation, see David Sorkin, *The Transformation of German Jewry, 1780–1840*, Oxford: Oxford University Press, 1987.

3 Ernst Pawel, *The Labyrinth of Exile*, p. 13.

4 *Ibid.*, pp. 14ff.

5 That Magyar and German loyalties need not necessarily conflict can best be understood as a result of the alliance, going back at least to 1848, between German *liberal* culture and Magyar political *liberalism*, against the Habsburgs and their *Austrian* supporters, among whom were many German-speaking elements, including the Germans of Buda, but *not* the *liberal* German Jews of Pest. On Herzl's strong Magyar identity while in Pest, see Handler, *passim*.

6 Herzl's *Nationale* 1878–82 are in the Universitätsarchiv, Vienna.

7 Arthur Schnitzler, *Jugend in Wien: eine Autobiographie*, Frankfurt am Main, Fischer, 1981, p. 153.

8 See William McGrath, *Dionysian Art and Populist Politics in Austria*, New Haven, Yale University Press, 1974.

9 Pawel, pp. 16–18.

10 On anti-Semitism in Austria, see Peter Pulzer, *The Rise of Political anti-Semitism in Germany and Austria*, London, Peter Halban, 1988, rev. edn.

11 Theodor Herzl, *Briefe und Tagebücher*, vol. 1, pp. 608–15.
12 Pawel, pp. 69–70; Herzl, *Briefe und Tagebücher*, pp. 125–7.
13 Klaus Dethloff (ed.), *Theodor Herzl*, pp. 14ff.
14 Pawel, p. 120.
15 Amos Elon, *Herzl*, pp. 32ff.; Robert Wistrich, *The Jews of Vienna in the Age of Franz Joseph*, pp. 439–40.
16 Cf. Peter Loewenberg, 'Theodor Herzl: a psychoanalytic study in charismatic political leadership', pp. 166–7.
17 Pawel, pp. 109–10; Herzl, *Briefe und Tagebücher*, vol. 1, p. 499.
18 Herzl, *Briefe und Tagebücher*, vol. 2, p. 92.
19 Pawel, pp. 110–11, 139–43.
20 Stefan Zweig, *Die Welt von Gestern*, Frankfurt am Main, Fischer, 1970, pp. 131–2.
21 Cf. Steven Beller, *Vienna and the Jews, 1867–1938*.
22 Herzl, *Briefe und Tagebücher*, vol. 1, p. 212.
23 *Ibid.*, vol. 2, p. 44.
24 Pawel, p. 138.
25 Alex Bein, *Theodore Herzl*, pp. 57–60.
26 Herzl, *Briefe und Tagebücher*, vol. 2, p. 45.
27 Bein, p. 70.

2: *Parisian Premonitions*

1 'Der Feind der Gesetze', in Theodor Herzl, *Das Palais Bourbon*, pp. 73–88; cf. Dethloff, pp. 157–68.
2 Cf. Alex Bein, 'Some early Herzl letters', in *Herzl Yearbook*, vol. 1, pp. 302–4.
3 Herzl, *Briefe und Tagebücher*, vol. 1, pp. 499, 508, 527.
4 Cited in Elon, p. 112.
5 See 'Die Schule der Journalisten', in Herzl, *Palais Bourbon*, pp. 240–6; cf. Herzl, *Briefe und Tagebücher*, vol. 2, p. 114.
6 'Die Glosse' is reprinted in Dethloff, pp. 71–93.
7 See Wistrich, pp. 441–2.
8 Pawel, pp. 163–70; Wistrich, p. 374.
9 Bein, p. 83.
10 *Ibid.*, pp. 79–80.
11 Herzl, *Briefe und Tagebücher*, vol. 2, p. 45.
12 *Ibid.*, vol. 2, p. 46; cf. *Ibid.*, vol. 1, p. 508.
13 Cf. Herzl's comments to Sidney Whitman on the Dreyfus Affair: 'there could be no question as to the innocence of Dreyfus, but it would be nevertheless unwise to lose sight of the fact that certain aggressive Jewish elements were partly responsible for the Jews

having incurred hatred among a people which in times gone by had been most liberal in its treatment of his race.' In Sidney Whitman, *Things I Remember: the recollections of a political writer in the capitals of Europe*, London, Cassell, 1916, pp. 43–5.

14 Pawel, pp. 170–3. Cf. Herzl, *Palais Bourbon*, for Herzl's scepticism about French politics.

15 Cited in Leon Kellner, *Theodor Herzls Lehrjahre*, Vienna, Löwit, 1920, pp. 140–1.

16 Herzl, *Briefe und Tagebücher*, vol. 1, pp. 505–6; vol. 2, p. 46.

17 *Ibid.*, vol. 1, pp. 506–8.

18 *Ibid.*, vol. 1, pp. 511–24.

19 *Ibid.*, vol. 2, p. 113.

20 *Ibid.*, vol. 2, pp. 46–8.

21 Herzl, *Palais Bourbon*, p. 37.

22 Herzl, *Briefe und Tagebücher*, vol. 1, pp. 532–6.

23 *Ibid.*, vol. 2, pp. 48–51.

24 *Ibid.*, vol. 2, p. 51.

25 Pawel, pp. 198–9.

26 Herzl, *Briefe und Tagebücher*, vol. 1, p. 569; vol. 2, p. 50.

27 Theodor Herzl, *Das neue Ghetto*, pp. 35–6.

28 *Neue Freie Presse*, 16 January 1898, p. 1, morning edn.

29 Herzl, *Neue Ghetto*, p. 40.

30 *Ibid.*, pp. 28–30.

31 *Ibid.*, pp. 74–5.

32 Herzl's reason for anonymity has a certain Freudian under-current, for he explained to his confidant that in this instance, even more than at other times, he wanted 'to hide my sexual organs'. The German word he uses here is 'Geschlechtsteile', which is interesting because the word 'Geschlecht' can also be used to mean 'race', and was used in this way by Moritz Benedikt in his scolding of Herzl in 1893. That *The New Ghetto* was written partly as a response to Herzl's being identified as a Jew by his 'racial parts'—his beard and nose—seems to suggest that Herzl is also trying to hide his racial origins in his anonymity.

33 Herzl, *Briefe und Tagebücher*, vol. 1, pp. 557–62.

34 Theodor Herzl, *Zionistische Schriften*, p. 257.

35 Michael R. Marrus, *The Politics of Assimilation: the French Jewish community at the time of the Dreyfus Affair*, Oxford, Clarendon Press, 1971, p. 213.

36 Herzl, *Briefe und Tagebücher*, vol. 2, pp. 769 (notes for Hirsch), 158 (speech to the Rothschilds), and 103 where Herzl envisages

addressing the Palais Bourbon on the unfitness of Jews as soldiers: 'And the peoples cannot surrender themselves by making the members of an undigested and indigestible group the leaders of their armies.' See also note 13 above.

37 Herzl, *Briefe und Tagebücher*, vol. 2, pp. 51-5. On Viennese politics, see Beller, pp. 193ff.

3: The State of the Jews

1 Herzl, *Briefe und Tagebücher*, vol. 2, p. 136.
2 *Ibid.*, p. 86.
3 Herzl's description of the Hirsch meeting is in *Briefe und Tagebücher*, vol. 2, pp. 55-6; the notes for the meeting are in *ibid.*, pp. 760-70.
4 *Ibid.*, p. 764.
5 *Ibid.*, p. 65.
6 *Ibid.*, p. 769.
7 *Ibid.*, p. 769; see also pp. 103, 158. Cf. Herzl, *Judenstaat*, pp. 11, 21. See also note 37, chapter 2, above.
8 Herzl, *Briefe und Tagebücher*, vol. 2, p. 770.
9 Herzl, *Zionistische Schriften*, p. 9.
10 These notes can be found in Herzl, *Briefe und Tagebücher*, vol. 2, pp. 52-152.
11 *Ibid.*, p. 104.
12 *Ibid.*, p. 72.
13 Cf. Theodor Herzl, *Philosophische Erzählungen*, pp. 253-65.
14 Herzl, *Briefe und Tagebücher*, vol. 2, p. 91.
15 *Ibid.*, pp. 67, 69, 77, 102, 120.
16 *Ibid.*, pp. 81, 88, 131-2, 141.
17 *Ibid.*, pp. 70, 75, 81, 89, 92-4.
18 *Ibid.*, pp. 124, 127; on state socialism, cf. Joseph Adler, *The Herzl Paradox*, pp. 7-27.
19 Herzl, *Briefe und Tagebücher*, vol. 2, pp. 81, 129, 133.
20 *Ibid.*, p. 225.
21 *Ibid.*, pp. 152-201.
22 *Ibid.*, p. 197.
23 *Ibid.*, p. 155.
24 *Ibid.*, p. 200.
25 *Ibid.*, p. 65.
26 Cf. the emancipatory work by Salomon Hermann Mosenthal, *Deborah*, Leipzig, Reclam, 1908 (1849), where the Jew, Ruben, dismisses the idea of returning to Jerusalem as 'a religious fairy-

tale', p. 62. Austria is the true home, although Ruben is emigrating to America.

27 Theodor Herzl, *Judenstaat*, pp. 3–4.

28 *Ibid.*, pp. 5–6.

29 Arthur Hertzberg (ed.), *The Zionist Idea*, pp. 47–8.

30 Herzl, *Judenstaat*, pp. 7–18.

31 *Ibid.*, pp. 19–30.

32 *Ibid.*, pp. 31–64.

33 The following theory is also applied to an existing state, France, in 'Die Schule der Journalisten', in Herzl, *Palais Bourbon*, pp. 243ff.

34 Herzl, *Judenstaat*, pp. 65–71.

35 *Ibid.*, pp. 71–80.

36 *Ibid.*, pp. 81–6.

37 Herzl sometimes contemplated a racial definition, but at others rejected it as unrealistic; see *Briefe und Tagebücher*, vol. 2, pp. 210, 281.

38 Herzl, *Judenstaat*, p. 14.

39 *Ibid.*, pp. 63–4.

40 *Ibid.*, p. 56.

41 *Ibid.*, p. 58.

42 *Ibid.*, p. 74.

43 *Ibid.*, p. 70.

44 *Ibid.*, pp. 7–10, 78–80.

45 Herzl, *Briefe und Tagebücher*, vol. 2, p. 139.

46 Cf. Joseph Adler, 'Herzl's philosophy of new humanism', in *Herzl Yearbook*, vol. 3 (1960), pp. 175ff.; W. J. Cahnman, 'Adolf Fischhof and his Jewish followers', in *Leo Baeck Institute Yearbook* (1959), pp. 111–42.

47 Adler, *The Herzl Paradox*, pp. 7–15.

48 Dethloff, p. 34.

49 I owe this important idea to a suggestion of David Sorkin, St Antony's College, Oxford.

50 Herzl, *Judenstaat*, pp. 75–6.

51 *Ibid.*, p. 86.

52 Cf. Hertzberg, pp. 19, 134.

4: Political Life

1 Herzl, *Briefe und Tagebücher*, vol. 2, p. 100.

2 *Ibid.*, pp. 67, 95, 137.

3 *Ibid.*, p. 201.

4 *Ibid.*, pp. 254–7.
5 *Ibid.*, p. 294; Herzl, *Zionistische Schriften*, p. 265.
6 See Herzl, *Briefe und Tagebücher*, vol. 2, p. 332.
7 *Ibid.*, p. 635.
8 *Ibid.*, vol. 3, p. 378.
9 *Ibid.*, vol. 2, p. 537.
10 *Ibid.*, p. 570; vol. 3, pp. 291, 335.
11 *Ibid.*, vol. 2, pp. 538–9.
12 Cf. Schorske's often quoted article, 'Politics in a new key: an Austrian trio', in Carl E. Schorske, *Fin-de-siècle Vienna*, pp. 116–180, esp. 146–175.
13 Herzl, *Briefe und Tagebücher*, vol. 2, p. 65.
14 *Ibid.*, vol. 3, p. 129.
15 *Ibid.*, vol. 2, pp. 69, 214.
16 *Ibid.*, p. 554.
17 *Ibid.*, p. 725.
18 *Ibid.*, p. 129.
19 *Ibid.*, pp. 177, 186.
20 *Ibid.*, vol. 2, pp. 259, 397, 584; vol. 3, p. 178.
21 Schorske, pp. 200–1.
22 Herzl, *Briefe und Tagebücher*, vol. 2, p. 389.
23 *Ibid.*, p. 409.
24 *Ibid.*, p. 230.
25 *Ibid.*, p. 89.
26 *Ibid.*, p. 558.
27 *Ibid.*, pp. 624, 584, 206.
28 See Herzl's opening speech to the Second Congress, in Herzl, *Sechs Kongressreden*, pp. 19, 28.
29 *Ibid.*, p. 14; Herzl, *Zionistische Schriften*, p. 160.
30 Herzl, *Briefe und Tagebücher*, vol. 2, p. 127.
31 *Ibid.*, p. 341.
32 See Dethloff, pp. 178–85.
33 Herzl, *Briefe und Tagebücher*, vol. 2, p. 99.
34 *Ibid.*, p. 224.
35 *Ibid.*, p. 539.
36 *Ibid.*, vol. 3, p. 114.
37 *Ibid.*, vol. 2, p. 297.
38 Herzl, *Zionistische Schriften*, pp. 64–5.
39 *Ibid.*, p. 259.
40 Herzl, *Briefe und Tagebücher*, vol. 2, pp. 124, 241.
41 *Ibid.*, p. 288.
42 *Ibid.*, p. 545.

43 Herzl, *Zionistische Schriften*, pp. 196–9.
44 Herzl, *Briefe und Tagebücher*, vol. 3, p. 36.
45 Cf. Herzl's identification with Moses, *ibid.*, vol. 2, p. 575.
46 *Ibid.*, p. 305; Herzl, *Sechs Kongressreden*, p. 8.
47 Herzl, *Briefe und Tagebücher*, vol. 2, p. 730.
48 *Ibid.*, p. 391.
49 Karl Kraus, *Eine Krone für Zion* (Vienna, Moriz Frisch, 1898); Arthur Schnitzler, *Der Weg ins Freie*, Frankfurt am Main, Fischer, 1961, orig. publ. 1908.
50 Herzl, *Zionistische Schriften*, pp. 172–6.
51 On the history of Zionism before Herzl, see David Vital, *The Origins of Zionism*; Walter Laqueur, *A History of Zionism*; Hertzberg, *The Zionist Idea*; Shlomo Avineri, *The Making of Modern Zionism*.
52 Herzl, *Briefe und Tagebücher*, vol. 2, p. 286.
53 Herzl, *Zionistische Schriften*, pp. 157ff.
54 Herzl, *Sechs Kongressreden*, pp. 26, 48; *Zionistische Schriften*, p. 149; *Briefe und Tagebücher*, vol. 2, p. 657; vol. 3, p. 184.
55 Herzl, *Briefe und Tagebücher*, vol. 3, p. 117.
56 Conor Cruise O'Brien, *Parnell and his Party, 1880–1890* (Oxford, Clarendon Press, 1968), pp. 6–10, 347–56; F. S. L. Lyons, *Charles Stewart Parnell* (Oxford, Oxford University Press, 1977), pp. 608–20.
57 Herzl, *Sechs Kongressreden*, pp. 8–9, 61; *Briefe und Tagebücher*, vol. 2, pp. 222, 244.
58 Herzl, *Briefe und Tagebücher*, vol. 2, p. 384.
59 *Ibid.*, p. 134.
60 *Ibid.*, p. 306.
61 Herzl, *Sechs Kongressreden*, pp. 30–1.
62 Herzl, *Briefe und Tagebücher*, vol. 2, pp. 675–87.

5: *Altneuland*

1 Herzl, *Zionistische Schriften*, p. 265.
2 Herzl, *Briefe und Tagebücher*, vol. 2, pp. 208, 213–16, 243.
3 *Ibid.*, pp. 571–2.
4 *Ibid.*, p. 575.
5 *Ibid.*, vol. 3, pp. 131, 225.
6 *Ibid.*, pp. 461, 399.
7 *Ibid.*, p. 43.
8 I owe this insight to David Sorkin, of St Antony's College, Oxford; also cf. Bein, *Herzl*, pp. 396–7.

9 This is also, probably, a note of gratitude to Herzl's long-time patron, Friedrich II, Grand Duke of Baden.

10 Herzl, *Altneuland*, pp. 244–5.

11 *Ibid.*, p. 203.

12 'Let nothing human be alien to me.' *Ibid.*, p. 286.

13 *Ibid.*, pp. 287–91.

14 *Ibid.*, p. 15.

15 *Ibid.*, p. 18.

16 *Ibid.*, p. 120.

17 *Ibid.*, pp. 217–65.

18 *Ibid.*, p. 56.

19 *Ibid.*, p. 272.

20 *Ibid.*, p. 300.

21 *Ibid.*, p. 313.

22 *Ibid.*, p. 127.

23 *Ibid.*, p. 192–4. This idea was a verbatim transferral of Oscar Marmorek's plan as reported in Herzl's diary; see *Briefe und Tagebücher*, vol. 3, p. 124.

24 Herzl, *Briefe und Tagebücher*, vol. 3, pp. 38–9.

25 See Alex Bein, 'Franz Oppenheimer and Theodor Herzl', in *Herzl Yearbook*, vol. 4 (1961–2), pp. 71ff.

26 Herzl, *Altneuland*, p. 251.

27 *Ibid.*, p. 112.

28 *Ibid.*, p. 335; cf. Adler, *The Herzl Paradox*, pp. 7–36, 102–10. On early German nationalist social thought in Austria and the influence of Stein, see McGrath, *Dionysian Art*, pp. 36ff.

29 *Altneuland*, p. 102.

30 *Ibid.*, p. 88.

31 *Ibid.*, p. 103.

32 *Ibid.*, p. 314; cf. A. J. P. Taylor, *English History, 1914–1945* London, Penguin, 1970, pp. 25ff.

33 See Sorkin, *Transformation of German Jewry*, pp. 112ff.

34 Herzl, *Altneuland*, pp. 137–41.

35 *Ibid.*, pp. 324, 328.

36 *Ibid.*, p. 296.

37 *Ibid.*, pp. 74–5, 297.

38 *Ibid.*, pp. 154–74.

39 Herzl, *Briefe und Tagebücher*, vol. 3, p. 553.

40 Herzl, *Altneuland*, p. 318.

41 Areopagus was the site of the judicial council in Athens.

42 Herzl, *Altneuland*, pp. 252–65.

43 *Ibid.*, p. 298.

6: *Struggle for the Future*

1 Bein, *Herzl*, p. 518.
2 Quoted in Pawel, *Labyrinth*, p. 453.
3 Bein, pp. 405–9, Pawel, pp. 471–2.
4 Bein, pp. 408–10; Pawel, pp. 472–4.
5 Bein, p. 375.
6 Pawel, pp. 452–3.
7 Cf. David Vital, *Zionism*, pp. 357–8.
8 For what follows, see Bein, pp. 412ff.
9 Herzl, *Briefe und Tagebücher*, vol. 3, p. 183.
10 *Ibid.*, p. 408.
11 *Ibid.*, p. 564.
12 Quoted in Bein, p. 444.
13 Herzl, *Briefe und Tagebücher*, vol. 3, p. 464.
14 Bein, pp. 444–6; on Uganda see also Vital, *Zionism*, pp. 267–347; Michael Heymann (ed.), *The minutes of the Zionist General Council: the Uganda controversy* (Jerusalem, Israel Universities, 1970), vol. 1, pp. 14–39; vol. 2, pp. 5–93.
15 Letter to Nordau, 19.7.1903, quoted in Bein, p. 445.
16 Herzl, *Sechs Kongressreden*, pp. 69–81.
17 Cf. Chaim Weizmann, *Trial and Error*, vol. 1, pp. 83ff.
18 Bein, p. 464.
19 Herzl, *Briefe und Tagebücher*, vol. 3, pp. 606–7.
20 *Ibid.*, p. 626.
21 *Ibid.*, p. 610.
22 Bein, pp. 470–6.
23 Herzl, *Briefe und Tagebücher*, vol. 3, p. 626.
24 Bein, pp. 477–8.
25 *Ibid.*, p. 489.
26 *Ibid.*, pp. 492–8; cf. Vital, *Zionism*, pp. 342–5.
27 *Neue Freie Presse*, 7 July 1904, p. 1, morning edn.
28 Zweig, *Welt von Gestern*, p. 133.
29 Pawel, pp. 532ff.; Stewart, *Herzl*, pp. 338ff.
30 On Zionist politics after Herzl, see Laqueur, *Zionism*, pp. 136ff.

7: *Conclusion*

1 Herzl, *Briefe und Tagebücher*, vol. 3, p. 648.
2 *Ibid.*, p. 652.
3 Cf. Loewenberg, 'Herzl', pp. 151–2, 178.

4 Hannah Arendt, *Die verborgene Tradition*, Frankfurt, Suhrkamp, 1976, pp. 81ff.

5 Herzl, *Altneuland*, pp. 262–4.

6 *Ibid.*, pp. 119, 287.

7 Cf. Jacques Kornberg, 'Theodore Herzl: a re-evaluation', p. 226; Wistrich, *Jews of Vienna*, pp. 421ff.

8 Cf. Conor Cruise O'Brien, *The Siege*, pp. 18–20, 103.

9 Hertzberg, *The Zionist Idea*, pp. 46ff.

10 The debate is to be found in Douglas Villiers (ed.), *Next Year in Jerusalem: Jews in the twentieth century*, London, Douglas Villiers, 1976, pp. 98–106.

11 Bein, pp. 517–18; Adler, pp. 139ff.

12 Herzl, *Briefe und Tagebücher*, vol. 3, p. 43.

13 Pawel, *Labyrinth*, p. 406.

14 Laqueur, p. 133; also Avineri, pp. 99–100.

15 Cf. Kornberg, p. 248; Herzl, *Briefe und Tagebücher*, vol. 2, pp. 117ff. Herzl in 1895 envisaged, probably in a South American context, a 'benevolent expropriation' of the native populace by secret land purchase before settlement began. This, however, was a fleeting idea of his initial 'inspiration', not the basis of his later policy.

16 Cf. Arthur Hertzberg, *The Jews in America: four centuries of an uneasy encounter: a history*, New York, Simon & Schuster, 1989, pp. 384ff.; Jacob Neusner, *Who, Where and What is 'Israel'?: Zionist perspectives on Israeli and American Judaism*, Lanham, University Press, 1989, *passim*, esp. pp. 113–30.

17 Herzl, *Briefe und Tagebücher*, vol. 2, p. 191.

BIOGRAPHICAL NOTES

Adler, Victor (1852–1918). Born in Prague. Leader of German Nationalist students during Herzl's university years, and co-author of the Linz Programme. Later leader of Austrian socialism.

Ahad Ha'am (Asher Ginsberg) (1858–1927). Born in Odessa. A central figure in the Jewish renaissance, especially in his advocacy of Hebrew; leader in spirit of 'cultural Zionism', he was Herzl's chief polemical adversary.

Bacher, Eduard (1846–1908). Born in Postelberg, Bohemia. Joint chief editor of the *Neue Freie Presse*, and Herzl's boss.

Benedikt, Moritz (1849–1920). Born in Kwanitz, Moravia. Joint chief editor, after 1908 sole chief editor, of the *Neue Freie Presse*. Held to be one of the most influential men in Austrian politics.

Birnbaum, Nathan (1864–1937). Born in Vienna. Precursor of Herzl. Inventor of the term 'Zionism'; founder of the first Jewish nationalist journal in German, *Selbstemanzipation* in 1885. Later a maverick in, and out, of the Zionist movement.

Buber, Martin (1878–1965). Born in Vienna, brought up in Lvov. One of the seminal Jewish thinkers of modern times; a leading figure in the 'cultural Zionist' opposition to Herzl.

Chamberlain, Joseph (1836–1914). Leading Liberal, then 'Unionist', English politician. As Colonial Secretary (1895–1903), made the Uganda offer to Herzl.

Cowen, Joseph (1868–1932). English Zionist; one of Herzl's favourites; model for Jo Levy in *Altneuland*.

Daudet, Alphonse (1840–97). Prominent French writer with anti-Semitic sympathies; acquaintance of Herzl during his Paris years.

Drumont, Edouard (1844–1917). Leading French anti-Semite; author of *La France juive* and publisher of *La Libre Parole*, he broke the Panama Scandal and was deeply involved in the Dreyfus Affair.

Feiwel, Berthold (1875–1937). Born in Pohrlitz, Moravia. An ardent supporter of Herzl (appointed editor of *Die Welt* in 1901), before gravitating to the cultural Zionist opposition, becoming one of its leaders.

Friedjung, Heinrich (1851–1920). German Nationalist as a young man, and co-author of the Linz Programme; later a prominent liberal historian. The model for one of Herzl's plans for his Zionist novel.

Friedrich II, Grand Duke of Baden (1826–1907). Uncle of Emperor Wilhelm II; monarch of Germany's most liberal and democratic state; provided Herzl's entrée to German ruling circles.

Goldsmid, Col. Albert Edward (1864–1904). Born in Bombay, brought up a Christian; became an English army officer; returned to Judaism at age 24. Leading pre-Herzlian 'lover of Zion' in England; later somewhat ambivalent supporter of Herzl.

Greenberg, Leopold (1861–1931). British publisher; came to Zionism due to Herzl. Important role as negotiator with British government from 1902. From 1907 publisher of the *Jewish Chronicle*.

Güdemann, Rabbi Moritz (1835–1918). Official religious leader of Vienna's Jewish community; originally impressed by Herzl and his plan, he became a major opponent of Zionism.

Hechler, William (1845–1931). Anglican priest, with messianic leanings; arranged Herzl's meeting with the Grand Duke of Baden, and influential in German court circles.

Hertzka, Theodor (1845–1924). Born in Budapest; became a Viennese journalist; author of *Freiland* (1889), a quasi-socialist Utopian novel centred on the idea of land communalism. This novel was cited, and criticized, by Herzl in *Der Judenstaat*.

Hess, Moses (1812–75). Born in Bonn. Originally a socialist, he became a precursor of Zionism. His book, *Rome and Jerusalem* (1862) anticipates many of Herzl's arguments.

Hirsch, Maurice de (1831–96). Railway magnate, banker, and Jewish philanthropist; founder of the Jewish Colonization Association; financed Jewish colonies in Argentina. The man Herzl first approached with his 'idea'.

Kraus, Karl (1874–1936). Born in Jicin, Bohemia; a central figure of Viennese modern culture around 1900; author of the satire directed against Herzl, *Eine Krone für Zion* (1898).

Lassalle, Ferdinand (1825–64). Born in Breslau; one of the founding fathers of German socialism, he advocated a form of state socialism, and was a strong Prussian patriot. One of Herzl's heroes.

Leitenberger, Baron Friedrich (1837–99). Viennese, Christian manufacturer; co-founder of the League for the Defence against Anti-Semitism; correspondent of Herzl in early 1893.

Lesseps, Ferdinand de (1805–94). Visionary engineer, builder of the Suez Canal; Herzl's boyhood idol, he was later at the centre of the Panama Scandal.

Lueger, Karl (1844–1910). Leader of the anti-Semitic Christian Social Party, and mayor of Vienna from 1897 until his death.

Menger, Anton (1841–1906). Legal theorist, professor in Vienna's Law Faculty, where Herzl was a student; sympathetic to the 'academic socialists', and a strong advocate of the state's role in ensuring social justice.

Nevlinski, Philip Michael de (1841–99). Polish nobleman, diplomat, spy and confidence trickster. Herzl's first main contact with the Turkish government.

Nordau, Max (1849–1923). Hungarian-born. Resident in Paris from 1880, he became famous as a social and cultural critic for books such as *Degeneration* (1893). From the start Herzl's faithful lieutenant in the Zionist movement; as a German-speaking Hungarian Jew, Nordau agreed with Herzl in his assessment of cultural Zionism, and led the counter-attack on Ahad Ha'am in 1902. .

Oppenheimer, Franz (1864–1943). Born in Berlin. A disciple of Theodor Hertzka (see above), he developed plans for Jewish land communes similar to that described by Herzl in *Altneuland*.

Pinsker, Leon (1821–91). From Odessa; a leader of the *Hibbat Zion* movement, and the author of *Autoemancipation* (1882), an early Zionist tract.

Plehve, Vyacheslav (1846–1904). Russian Minister of the Interior at the time of the Kishinev pogrom, whom Herzl nevertheless went to meet in 1903.

Rothschild, Baron Salomon Albert (1844–1911). Head of the Viennese branch of the family; he did not reply to Herzl's letter in 1895.

Rothschild, Baron Edmond de (1845–1934). Member of the Parisian branch of the family; philanthropist and founder of Jewish colonies in Palestine. While he granted Herzl an interview in 1896 he refused to support Herzl's plans.

Rothschild, Nathaniel Meyer, Lord (1840–1915). Head of the London branch; responded positively, if guardedly, to Herzl in 1902 over the El Arish project.

Schnitzler, Arthur (1861–1931). Born in Vienna; a central figure of *fin-de-siècle* Vienna, he acted as Herzl's confidant in the early 1890s. He did not agree with Zionism, however, as his *Der Weg ins Freie* (1908) makes clear.

Schönerer, Georg von (1842–1921). Leader of radical German Nationalism in Austria, and a vehement racial anti-Semite.

Speidel, Ludwig (1830–1906). Influential theatre critic, and colleague of Herzl's at the *Neue Freie Presse*.

Stein, Lorenz von (1815–90). One of Herzl's law professors; a Hegelian who, while rejecting socialism, advocated a role for the state in social amelioration.

Trietsch, Davis (1870–1935). Born in Dresden. Zionist; chief proponent of 'Greater Palestine', including Cyprus and El Arish.

Unger, Joseph (1828–1913). Austrian legal theorist; codifier of Austrian civil law; one of the most prominent liberal thinkers in Austria; converted Jew.

Ussishkin, Menachem (1863–1941). Born in Dubrovno, Russia; a leading Russian Zionist; Herzl's chief adversary in the struggle over Uganda; model for the Jewish peasant, Mendel in *Altneuland*.

Weizmann, Chaim (1874–1952). Born in Motol, Russia. A leader of the cultural Zionist opposition to Herzl, and later the leader of 'synthetic Zionism'. He played a central role in the bringing about of the Balfour Declaration of 1917. Israel's first president.

Wolffsohn, David (1856–1914). Lithuanian-born; became timber merchant in Cologne; early German Zionist, close supporter of Herzl and his chosen successor. 1905–11, president of the Zionist organization. Model for David Littwak in *Altneuland*.

Zangwill, Israel (1864–1926). Born in London. Prominent English Jewish writer. A supporter of Herzl from 1895, he was a leader of the 'Western' wing of Zionism, which stressed the 'normalizing' function of a state of the Jews. He led the secession from the Seventh Congress in 1905 to form the Jewish Territorialist Organization.

Zweig, Stefan (1881–1942). Austrian Jewish writer, and admiring acquaintance of Herzl.

SELECT BIBLIOGRAPHY

Works by Herzl in German

Altneuland, Leipzig, Seemann, 1902.
Briefe und Tagebücher, 3 vols to date, eds A. Bein, H. Greive, M. Schärf, J. H. Schoeps, Berlin, Propyläen, 1983.
Buch der Narrheit, Leipzig, Freund, 1888.
Feuilletons, 2 vols, with an introduction by Raoul Auernheimer, Berlin, Harz, 1911.
Der Judenstaat: Versuch einer modernen Lösung der Judenfrage, Vienna, Breitenstein, 1896.
Das neue Ghetto, Vienna, Selbstverlag, 1903.
Neues von der Venus, Leipzig, Freund, 1887.
Das Palais Bourbon: Bilder aus dem französichen Parlamentsleben, Leipzig, Duncker und Humblot, 1895.
Philosophische Erzählungen, Berlin, B. Harz, 1919 (orig. publ. 1900).
Sechs Kongressreden, Leipzig, 1914.
Zionistische Schriften, ed. L. Kellner, Berlin, Jüdischer Verlag, 1920.
A very useful collection of Herzl's works, with an excellent introductory essay, is K. Dethloff (ed.), *Theodor Herzl, oder der Moses des Fin de Siècle*, Vienna, Böhlau, 1986.

Works by Herzl in English

The Complete Diaries of Theodor Herzl, 5 vols, ed. R. Patai, trans. H. Zohn, New York, Yoseloff, 1960.
The Jewish State, trans. H. Zohn, New York, Herzl Press, 1970.
The New Ghetto, trans. H. Norden, New York, Herzl Foundation, 1955.
Old New Land, trans. L. Levensohn, New York, Bloch, 1960.
Zionist Writings: essays and addresses, 2 vols, trans. H. Zohn, New York, 1973.

Secondary Works in English

Adler, Joseph, *The Herzl Paradox: political, social and economic theories*

SELECT BIBLIOGRAPHY

of a realist, New York, Hadrian/Herzl Press, 1962.

Avineri, Shlomo, *The Making of Modern Zionism, the intellectual origins of the Jewish state*, New York, Basic Books, 1981.

Bein, Alex, *Theodore Herzl*, Philadelphia, Jewish Publication Society of America, 1941.

Beller, Steven, *Vienna and the Jews, 1867–1938: a cultural history*, Cambridge, Cambridge University Press, 1989.

Elon, Amos, *Herzl*, New York, Schocken, 1986.

Handler, Andrew, *Dori, the life and times of Theodor Herzl in Budapest (1860–1878)*, University of Alabama, 1983.

Hertzberg, Arthur (ed.), *The Zionist Idea: a historical analysis and reader*, New York, Atheneum, 1959.

Herzl Yearbook, New York, 1960– .

Kornberg, Jacques, 'Theodore Herzl, a re-evaluation', in *Journal of Modern History*, vol. 52, no. 2 (June 1980), pp. 226–52.

Laqueur, Walter, *A History of Zionism*, New York, Schocken, 1989.

Loewenberg, Peter, 'Theodor Herzl, a psychoanalytic study in charismatic political leadership', in Benjamin B. Wolman (ed.), *The Psychoanalytic Interpretation of History*, New York, Basic Books, 1971, pp. 150–91.

O'Brien, Conor Cruise, *The Siege: the saga of Israel and Zionism*, London, Weidenfeld & Nicolson, 1986.

Pawel, Ernst, *The Labyrinth of Exile: a life of Theodor Herzl*, New York, Farrar, Straus & Giroux, 1989.

Schorske, Carl E., *Fin-de-siècle Vienna: politics and culture*, London, Weidenfeld & Nicolson, 1979.

Stewart, Desmond, *Theodor Herzl: artist and politician: a biography of the father of modern Israel*, New York, Doubleday, 1974.

Vital, David, *The Origins of Zionism*, Oxford, Clarendon Press, 1975.

Vital, David, *Zionism: the formative years*, Oxford, Clarendon Press, 1982.

Weizmann, Chaim, *Trial and Error*, Philadelphia, Jewish Publication Society of America, 1949.

Wistrich, Robert, *The Jews of Vienna in the Age of Franz Joseph*, Oxford, Oxford University Press, 1989.

INDEX

INDEX

Mendelssohn
David Sorkin

Moses Mendelssohn (1729–1786) was the premier Jewish thinker of his day and one of the best-known figures of the German Enlightenment, earning the sobriquet "the Socrates of Berlin". He was thoroughly involved in the central issue of Enlightenment religious thinking: the inevitable conflict between reason and revelation in an age concerned with individual rights and religious toleration.

Mendelssohn did not aspire to a comprehensive philosophy of Judaism, since he thought human reason was limited, but he did see Judaism as compatible with toleration and rights. He attempted to revive the practical tradition of medieval Jewish rationalism in philosophy and Biblical exegesis, and aimed to provide the practical knowledge that would aid piety and observance. David Sorkin offers a close study of Mendelssohn's complete writings, treating the German, and the often-neglected Hebrew writings, as a single corpus and arguing that Mendelssohn's two spheres of endeavour were entirely consistent.

"a first-rate introduction to the most important figure in modern Jewish thought . . . clearly structured and elegantly written" *Journal of Jewish Studies*

"Sorkin has established himself as one of the most insightful scholars of modern Jewish intellectual history"
David N. Myers, U.C.L.A.

Heine
Ritchie Robertson

Born in Düsseldorf at the end of the eighteenth century, Heinrich Heine (1797–1856) is now recognized as one of Germany's greatest writers of verse and prose. His writings are indebted in complex ways to both Classicism and Romanticism though his love-hate relation with Romanticism was particularly intense. Both, he felt, debarred the artist from dealing adequately with a modern world and both excluded politics. Heine was always acutely conscious of history and politics; Düsseldorf was part of the Napoleonic Empire during Heine's formative years and he grew up in a world changed forever by the French Revolution.

Heine's agile mind and brilliant wit expressed themselves in lyric and satiric verse, travel writing and essays on literature, art, politics and history. He was a great satirist and thinker—but not a philosopher. One of his most perceptive admirers, Nietzsche, said of him, 'He possessed that divine malice without which perfection, for me, is unimaginable.'

One of the great ambivalences in Heine's life was his attitude to being a German Jew in the age of partial emancipation. Amongst Heine's friends was Moses Mendelssohn, the philosopher of the *Haskulah*—the Jewish Enlightenment—but Heine's own attitude to Judaism was far from straightforward. He himself converted to Protestantism but deplored his conversion and forever bitterly regretted it.

Bialik
David Aberbach

During his lifetime, Chaim Nachman Bialik was hailed as the poet laureate of Jewish nationalism and was regarded as one of the major Jewish cultural influences of his age. He was seen as the poet of hope and revival in an age which witnessed the Russian Pale of Settlement, pogroms, the Russian Revolution, the rise of Zionism and of Hebrew as a living language.

David Aberbach explores the historical, social and literary background to Bialik's rise as a Romantic-nationalist poet, his ambivalence to this national role, his obsession with intensely private themes and the interplay between the public figure and the confessional lyric poet.

Aberbach shows how Bialik's poetry reveals a profoundly tortured inner life and how strongly he felt the inseparable links between his art and his life.

Ibn Gabirol
Raphael Loewe

Solomon ibn Gabirol (*c.* 1021–*c.* 1070), possibly the greatest of all the Spanish-Jewish poets, was also a neoplatonic philosopher of importance and known to Christian scholasticim as Avicebrol. The virtuosity of Gabirol's Hebrew—so apparent in his poetry—matches a brilliance in biblical allusion and reveals something of the social history of the period and of Ibn Gabirol's own profound spirituality.

His philosophical treatise—written in Arabic—is entitled in its Hebrew translation *Meqor Ḥayyim* (*Fountain of Life*). It expounds a theory of creation based on the relationship of matter to form. His extensive Hebrew poem entitled *Kether Malkuth* (*Royal Crown*) links theology, cosmology, and psychology and appears here in a new English rendering in metaphysical verse by Raphael Loewe.

Ibn Gabirol's work links Jewish philosophy with the intellectual climate of Moorish Spain and has left its mark, through St Thomas Aquinas, on the thought of medieval Europe. His liturgical poetry has endowed Sephardi Jewry with some of the noblest pieces of its rich cultural heritage.

Rashi
Chaim Pearl

Rashi (Rabbi Solomon ben Isaac 1040–1105), was the greatest Jewish Bible commentator of all time. He brought to his exposition of the text of the Bible some of the vast treasury of rabbinic folklore, homily and ethical teaching, thus enabling readers to gain both an understanding of the literal meaning of the Scriptures and an appreciation of the deeper significance of the text as it was handed down through centuries of Jewish tradition.

Similarly, Rashi's commentaries on the Talmud made this work accessible and saved it from obscurity. Through his encyclopaedic knowledge he was able to explain the language, ideas and rabbinic discussions contained within the Talmud. The Bible and the Talmud always formed the core of Jewish learning and Rashi's commentaries immediately became an essential part of this learning.

This book discusses the life of Rashi and gives a lucid and full account of his monumental achievement against the rich background of 11th-century France.

Buber
Pamela Vermes

On 13 July, 1965 more than 2,000 people crammed into the memorial srvice for Martin Buber. Yet, during his lifetime, some had said his work was esoteric, impossible for most people to understand, and he was branded a dubious interpreter of Jewish values.

Who was he then, this gifted man whose studies ranged from philosophy to education, to psychology, to politics, to biblical studies and further? He denied that he was a philosopher or theologian. He refused to accept the feasibility of union with God—the declared aim of the mystic. His role was that of a guide rather than an instructor. 'I demonstrate reality,' he insisted. 'I have no doctrine, I conduct a conversation.' He found it intolerable that religion should be a thing apart, a sacred speciality, and called for the recognition of divine Presence in everyday life. From the Bible and from Hasidism, Buber, an existential interpreter, drew and reformulated truths which Jews and non-Jews alike recognize as necessary to the development and wholeness of the individual.

That he was a Zionist there is no doubt though he belonged to a minority which sought a compromise with the Palestinian Arabs. He abhorred bloodshed and sought a peaceful co-existence between the two peoples.

Ahad Ha'am
Steven J. Zipperstein

Ahad Ha'am was the pen name of Asher Ginzberg (1856–1927), a Russian Jew whose life intersected nearly every important trend and current in contemporary Jewry. His influence extended to figures as varied as the scholar of mysticism Gershom Scholem, the Hebrew poet Chaim Nachman Bialik , and the historian Simon Dubnow. Theodor Herzl may have been the political leader of the Zionist movement, but Ahad Ha'am exerted a rare, perhaps unequalled, authority within Jewish culture through his writings.

Ahad Ha'am was a Hebrew essayist of extraordinary knowledge and skill, a public intellectual who spoke with refreshing candour on every controversial issue of the day. He was the first Zionist to call attention to the issue of Palestinian Arabs. He was a critic of the use of aggression as a tool in advancing Jewish nationalism and a foe of clericalism in Jewish public life.

His analysis of the prehistory of Israeli political culture was incisive and prescient. Steven Zipperstein offers all those interested in contemporary Jewry, in Zionism, and in the ambiguities of modern nationalism a wide-ranging, perceptive reassessment of Ahad Ha'am's life against the back-drop of his contentious political world.

Arlosoroff
Shlomo Avineri

Chaim Arlosoroff (1899–1933), socialist Zionist leader and theorist, was born in Russia and educated in Germany. He was one of the leaders of the Labour Zionist Party, Mapai and, following his emgration to Palestine in the 1920s, he became the head of the political department of the Jewish Agency for Palestine—the 'Foreign Minister' of the Jewish state-in-the-making.

His reputation grew rapidly and his many articles and speeches were soon treated as blueprints for the socialist ideals of a Jewish state. He was bitterly opposed to the Revisionist principles of Jabotinsky and his movement. At the age of thirty-four, Arlosoroff was assassinated while walking with his wife along the beach in Tel Aviv. His murder marked a turning point in modern Zionist history, polarizing attitudes between left- and right-wing Zionists in Palestine and the Diaspora, and creating an ideological rift parallel only to the impact of the Dreyfus Affair on French politics.

After his death, Arlosoroff became a symbol of the socialist Zionist movement. He was an intellectual of the first order and an original social thinker. He had a number of books to his name in such fields as socialist and anarchist thought, economic history, Jewish social studies, financial theory and social analysis. His writings and ideas set the scene for the final struggle towards an independent Jewish state in Palestine and time has proved him to be extraordinarily prophetic.